This book is for

- You want to learn how to identify and be secure in your life's purpose and what it takes to harness your gifting to impact lives.
- You are busy with life and feel the need or stirring still to do more!
- You are keen to make more of your life so that society may be blessed through you!
- You are keen to make impact with your life but do not know how!
- You want to learn to make room for God to use your life, aspiring to do something for God!
- You want to leave a legacy of greatness, earning the right to history's recognition that you once lived!
- You crave the opportunity to do ministry in your marketplace – possessing the nations one encounter at a time!

Learn how a little gift of your space and time for His course yields great dividends for the kingdom and multiplies your avenue for impact!

This book is also for you if in the business of your life, you have had little time for God although you yearn for a richer and deeper walk with Him.

What people are saying...

In her book – Can God Interrupt your Life, Grace takes us on her personal journey – her joy in discovering that there is a "multiplicity of avenues" for impacting the lives of others with the Gospel of God's love. She shows that it is possible to pursue your career and also serve God full time!

As you read this book, you may identify with her as she clearly articulates her initial struggles in conforming to God's plan for her life. Grace challenges believers in various fields of professional practice to also respond to God's call and plan for their lives despite the inconveniences and the possible embarrassments that heeding to this call may lead to; a plan that may not entirely fit into your present lifestyle or agenda.

No doubt, a brilliant mind, articulating her line of thoughts with relevant analogies across various professional disciplines! It is practical, exciting and encouraging.

This book is a real time 21st century example for the contemporary believer from a writer who is herself a Senior Registrar, a Pastor's wife and a mother! You certainly will be blessed.

Reverend (Mrs) Pearl Ampofo
Associate Pastor, Gracefields Chapel Int.

My suggestion to anyone reading this book is that you set aside a dedicated time - sit, read, and after finishing it, sit and dwell on it a little more and let not just the words that Grace has written impact and challenge you but above all, let God minister through all these to you!

Each chapter does not just speak biblical truth but most important of all challenges one to think "how can I live out my life when God calls?"

As a doctor myself, I have always asked through my career, "Lord, how should Christians in the workplace behave?" When I met Grace, a fellow obstetrician, I saw God answering my question. Her life story, her obedience, and above all how she carries herself at work, emulates a role model for not just fellow Christians to look up to, but also for non-Christians to challenge and ask themselves what is so different about her and how can I be like her? I have also seen, through her allowing God to interrupt her life that yes, God does not promise that everything will be smooth-sailing, but if nothing at all, He provides and He blesses not just her but her family abundantly!

Dr Edwina Goh
Senior Registrar
(Obstetrics andGynaecology)

About the Author

Dr (Mrs) Grace Asante – Duah is a professional woman, wife, mother, writer and speaker. She has travelled extensively throughout the UK and abroad (Israel, Ukraine, USA) teaching the church and general public on health and speaking at various conferences.

She is an advocate for bringing excellence to every aspect of one's life, serving as an example in the community, a role model to the many that she interacts with.

As a medical doctor specialising in Obstetrics and Gynaecology, Grace exemplifies the multifaceted individual, effortlessly marrying the role of skilled clinician and surgeon, a leader, teacher of the word, wife and mother. She is actively engaged in the mentorship of the next generation, empowering young women in particular and the youth in general, to fulfil their God-given assignment and purpose for life.

In all these she lets through God's light, being a beacon to draw others to the Lord.

A minister's wife in the Church of Pentecost (COP UK), Grace is an active part of her husband, Rev Ernest Duah's ministry. They are blessed with two beautiful children, Danalyn and Joseph.

What people are saying...

"The idea of being a witness for Christ alongside having the attitude of being minister in the workplace is critical to the eternal impact a Christian professional has in the workplace. Grace Inspires us to commit to having an eternal perspective and an enduring impact on everyone we meet through our businesses or professional undertakings.

Grace's content and clarity on the subject of ministry in the marketplace is a clarion call to every Christian professional to step up to the plate and be counted - utilising every available opportunity as a platform for Christian ministry and showcase Christ - shining like stars in a crooked and depraved world.

- Albert Addai (Rev), Gracefields Chapel England.

CAN GOD INTERRUPT YOUR LIFE?

Acknowledgements

Thanks be to God who gives me life and gave the conception of this book the day He asked me, as if in exasperation at my numerous excuses regarding my husband's call into full-time ministry: "Grace, can I interrupt your life?" In the ensuing dialogue, over a seven-year period, He opened my eyes to understand that the practice of medicine (my calling) was but one of several vehicles for the fulfilment of my mandate as one made in His image.

I also wish to thank my husband, Pastor Ernest Kwame Duah (Church of Pentecost UK) through whom God elevated me to the status of wife and mother. In my union with you, I have discovered the multiplicity of avenues for the fulfilment of purpose – "be fruitful and multiply"!

Thank you Danalyn and Joseph Duah, my children; the two most precious beings in my world. Thank you for making me feel I own the world. You will not miss the fulfilment of your mandate in life.

My thanksgiving will not be complete without acknowledging the immense support I have enjoyed from my fathers in COP UK: Apostles Osei Owusu Afriyie (National Head), James Sam, George Korankye, Oheneba Appiah Bonna and Reverend Francis Owusu Kwaah (Area Heads), Apostle Kwaku Frempong Boadu (National Secretary) and their wives. I am also grateful to the entire pastorate of COP UK and their wives for every support given me in diverse ways. I also wish to thank, from the bottom of my heart my fathers in the Lord, Apostles M. S Appiah, Amos Jimmy Markin, N. A. O. Amergatcher, and Reverend Simon Ampofo (General Overseer - Gracefields Chapel) and their wives for the depth of mentorship and love. May the Lord continue to richly bless you!

My special appreciation goes to Mrs Rose Arthur (COP Ukraine) and Mrs Irene Wiafe (COP UK) who by their kindness and acceptance of me just as I am (faults and all) give me room to fit in. Thank you for leaving your doors open to me always!

Thank you Filament Publishing- Roy Francis who challenged my thinking through healthy discourse and Chris Day, who was ever so accommodating.

A very big thank you to Pastor (Professor) Kobby Koduah (VC, Pentecost University), Elder Osei Kuffour (Barrister at Law), and Deaconess Eunice Chemel- Addo (a.k.a. Lady Pastor) for their input in reading through the manuscript and critiquing it.

Mr Krobeah Asante Baah (dad) and Mrs Doris Susanna Amponsah Baah (mum): thank you for being my parents, teaching me first to know and to love the Lord, and then to serve Him whilst serving humankind.

I would like to acknowledge especially my brothers Martin, Acheamfour Yeboah, and Benjamin for always being there for me and to all the people I have encountered in life, who have shaped my faith and thinking in diverse ways – thank you!

Dedication:

This book is dedicated to
Mr Krobeah Asante Baah,
my dad, who showed me my Heavenly Father
by his earthly example.

CAN GOD INTERRUPT YOUR LIFE?

Dr (Mrs) Grace Asante-Duah

ॐ

Published by
Filament Publishing Ltd
16, Croydon Road, Beddington,
Croydon. Surrey CR0 4PA
+44(0)20 8688 2598
info@filamentpublishing.com
www.filamentpublishing.com

© 2021 Dr (Mrs) Grace Asante-Duah

ISBN 978-1-913623-32-6

The right of Dr (Mrs) Grace Asante-Duah to be identified as the author of this work has been asserted by her in accordance with the Designs and Copyrights Act 1988 Section 77

All rights reserved
No portion of this work may be copied by any means without the prior written permission of the publishers

Book editing - Mrs Rose Arthur
Printed in the UK by 4Edge
Cover Design by Pokes: 07961287360

Table of Contents

Foreword	12
Preface	15
Author's note	17
Chapter 1 – The Call: Back to the original design and purpose of man	23-41
Chapter 2 - Can God interrupt your life?	43-60
Chapter 3 – My willing availability	61-80
Chapter 4 - For such a time as this!	81-100
Chapter 5 - Unction to function: Empowered for the assignment	101-121
Chapter 6 - The Blessing of the fulfilled life	123-132
Chapter 7 – The consequences of the delayed response: Attend to your Nineveh!	133-148
Glossary	149

Foreword

Dr (Mrs) Grace Asante- Duah doubles as a Medical Doctor (Senior Registrar in Obstetrics and Gynaecology) and wife of a Minister of Religion in The Church of Pentecost, based in the United Kingdom. God has endowed her with the ability to diligently go about her medical practice as well as leading and teaching God's people, not just about health-related issues but also rightly dividing the word of truth. In the Church, one of her strengths is in the area of Worship. Her close relationship with the Lord has caused her to come out with this book which is of great importance not only to the Christian community but to all who are faced with the big question of where their life's trajectory and emphasis should be.

When faced with the question "Can God Interrupt Your Life?" it is very crucial for a person to understand that our existence on this earth came by the Almighty God. Undoubtedly, God, who made the heavens and earth and lastly made man, endowed humanity with a destiny. From the Scriptures, everything God made was handed over to mankind to oversee and even add to (Genesis 1: 28). Though God has given man a personal WILL power, He expects that His will which is perfect and supersedes man's should rather prevail on earth. Those who turn to God as their creator and seek guidance always see their way very clearly.

Unfortunately, when people make decisions, more often than not, they forget that there is an Omnipotent Being who can provide perfect direction to enable them to reach their destinations unscathed. As soon as there seems to be an interruption of their laid out plans for life somewhere along the line, they frown at it, thinking it is up to them to decide how their lives should be and that there should be no interferences. The Scripture in Proverbs 19:20- 21, plays a very vital role in this discourse:

> *"Listen to advice and accept instruction, and in the end you will be wise. Many are the plans in a man's heart, but it is the LORD'S purpose that prevails" (Proverbs 19: 20-21, NIV).*

Grace's statement that 'there is no one fixed way in which the Lord uses His children to be a blessing unto others" holds true. She further asserts that "often, God uses that which you have to hand as the first but not the only vehicle for the manifestation of His will and glory". That is what this timely book is about, communicating the impact that one's life can have when rendered open to the Lord for His use. If God is the potter and human beings are the clay, does He not have the right to shape what is marred in His hands into another pot as reflects in (Jeremiah 18: 1-6.)?

When you understand the deep knowledge, that God can interrupt our actions not for evil but good, the Holy Spirit will lead you to accomplish what is the purpose of God for your life.

In this book, Grace tries to convey a simple but powerful truth that will clear our minds. With simplicity, she divides the word of God, helping us to understand and accept the fact that, God's interruptions in our decision making and actions will, in the long run, lead us to accomplish the dreams we have and the goals we want to achieve.

Note that the plans of God for us are not destructive but for prosperity and hope.

Just be flexible in the hands of God and you will be glad He interrupted you.

Grace and Peace to you.

Martin Seth Appiah (Apostle)
The Area Head, the Church of Pentecost
Madina Area, Accra-Ghana

PREFACE

The popular saying that the two most important days in your life are the day you were born and the day you find out or discover why is what came to mind when I had a first glimpse of the book "Can God interrupt your life?" The day you were born is important because that is when you are ushered into life with all the attributes of a human being with the potential to become who you were meant to be. You do not have a choice in this day of birth because you do not determine it and you have no say when it should happen. The second important day however needs your effort to happen because you must play a part to reach the point of discovery.

The good news is that God our Creator knows both days and determines the first but gives us the choice to discover the second. Many people unfortunately do not necessarily make the effort to find out the second most important day in their lives and they pass through life without achieving what God intended them to be. Some people stumble into their purpose in life while others just flow with the tide of life to do whatever comes their way without bothering to change anything. There are however some who determinedly seek to discover their purpose, in life and when they find it, pursue it to a meaningful end. Such people develop themselves to fulfil their purpose and leave no stone unturned until they achieve whatever potential they discover as their purpose in life. They successfully contribute to make their world a better place and posterity always bless them for their efforts.

In this book, I find Dr. Grace Duah falls in the category of people who go out to seek and find the second most important day in their lives and make use of it to affect their world positively. Through the pages of Can God interrupt your life? she succeeds in engaging her readers to appreciate the need to make every effort to find their purpose in life. By way of her struggles to come to terms with what needs to be done amidst trying to reconcile her dreams with what is expected of her by the society in which she finds herself, she successfully provides the much-needed encouragement to anyone battling to find his or her place in life, not to give up.

"Can God interrupt your life"? also gives readers the right perspective of God in the lives of human beings by reminding us that God is our Creator and as such knows what is best for each of us. We save ourselves from unnecessary stress by deferring to Him to discover our purpose in life and for direction after the discovery. Jeremiah 29:11 sums it all up beautifully when God says: For I know the plans I have for you, plans for welfare and not for evil, to give you a future and a hope (RSV)

Can God interrupt your life? is a must-read for everyone who wants to make an impactful difference in life with the help of God, and not just merely pass through life aimlessly. I recommend it especially for women who come from cultures that try to subtly discourage women not to follow their dreams to achieve their purpose in life.

Dr. Abigail Kyei
Health & Management Consultant, Ghana

Author's Note

I have always considered the practice of medicine my calling, not just a profession or a career path. The journey culminating in becoming a Specialty Registrar in Obstetrics and Gynaecology started very early in my life.

I was only four years old, my mother tells me, when it became noticeable the penchant I had to try to administer some form of therapy toward healing the unwell. My mother kept chicken in our compound. Time and time again she would find me with a chick cushioned upon my lap, cradled in a kitchen towel being ministered to. I would mix the antibiotic contained in Amoxicillin capsules, which were easily accessible in Ghana (my land of birth), in water, and feed this solution to chicks in the house that had fallen ill. Most of these chicks got well and she observed the great pleasure and feeling of accomplishment I derived from it. When a chick didn't survive, she watched me upset and forlorn, because I really cared.

As this continued she thought it expedient to nurture this natural leaning and provided me with plastic replicas of a stethoscope, kidney dish, and sponge holding forceps. She describes how with great enjoyment, she watched me as I carried these items in a plastic bag with me wherever I went. I would tell anyone who would listen that I was going to be a doctor when I grew up and as I got older, l would specifically say that my hands were made for operating. These assertions remained constant she tells me, never once mentioning a different profession as something I desired to do.

In my mind there has always been great certainty that I am called to do what I do and that my medical practice is a way of ministering to others; God's pre-planned route for my life to be a blessing to others. When God came knocking at my door regarding another avenue or means by which to impact lives, I felt conflicted and overstretched. The perceived great inconvenience this additional demand on me was going to be and the demands of my life as it is felt an unmanageable blend. Would I need to quit my medical practice in order to pick up this new call? Or do I focus on my medical practice and continue to be a blessing in the capacity I had already? Was there room for taking up additional responsibilities without compromising current responsibilities such as the blend of family life and professional practice? What do I do?

This may most likely be a feeling that most people have about the endeavours they pursue in life and God. Sometimes, it may seem to leave no room for the desire that may exist to be used more of God to impact our society. Where we feel the stirring of God's call, can God interrupt our lives? What would it mean to us to do God's work and to leave our mark on society? What may be the price we pay? Is there any sacrifice involved and what benefit is there in giving your all to the Lord? These are the questions this book seeks to help answer. It seeks to give you a second opinion on the issue, whereby God's interruptions in our lives can become a welcome adventure of grace. The opportunity to serve would usually culminate in deep fulfilment, derived from a life lived in service to God and humankind.

It is a normal human phenomenon to seek to achieve something that society can recognise as good – something worth celebrating. You are not alone in that desire of the heart and mind. Most people seek this attainment via various professional or career pursuits. Others find fulfilment through trade, the raising of a family etcetera. Yet still, others find no definable route by which this may be achieved. For most individuals, a noteworthy aspiration remains an unattainable goal. It becomes a desire that waxes and wanes in strength in the mind without ever finding expression on the outside.

There are many reasons why this may be so. It could be for fear of failing! In an instinct to protect oneself from ridicule, it appears inaction is a better alternative. The world seems to enable more idleness by the focus placed on our failings when we attempt to excel. Our inaction may also stem from a lack of understanding of one's purpose in life, an inability to answer the question "why do I live?" Even more worryingly, it may stem from a comparison of oneself with others. In so doing we deem what we aspire for, an insignificant contributor to the rich fabric of human society and life.

Inertia in life is all too unfortunately a state that many of us find ourselves in for a great part of our earthly lives. The saying that a cemetery is a deposit place of rich talents whilst the land of the living is grossly impoverished is sadly true. Many have died, still carrying the rich aspirations and plans they had in their mind, without it having seen the light of day! That is quite saddening.

To have lived ought to never be enough. To have lived as one ought to should be a goal all humankind strive for. And while this applies to all, it is more so for the child of God. When one has come to the saving knowledge of Christ, it becomes imperative that one's very life becomes a conduit of channelling the greatness of our God.

To my knowledge, there is no one fixed way in which the Lord uses His children to be a blessing to others. Often, He uses that which you have to hand. The daily activities of one's life become the opportunities one has. These may serve as the first, but not the only vehicle for the manifestation of His will and glory. In being a teacher, farmer, pharmacist, nurse, lawyer, actor, or mason, God can use you to be a blessing to others. Whether one is a carpenter, hairdresser, petty trader, or business person etcetera, in that lies the opportunity to be a blessing and to make an impact with your life. So long as God is allowed room to use your pursuits as a channel for His glory, your life becomes a conduit for His grace and mercy to the world.

We often misconstrue doing God's work as that which pastors and prophets do. The truth is that in every endeavour in life, His light can shine through us so long as we are willing for God to use what we have to hand. Whilst we are fixated on what we want in life and on doing things how we want to for the purposes we want, our lives remain on a self – directed course. Oftentimes, we are left with no substantial impact on our society in this way. When we yield our lives and the things we pursue to God for His use, we are effectively saying "feel free to interrupt my life, Lord".

Whether one is constantly in pursuit of life goals, be it benevolent or for personal gratification or you find yourself unengaged in the enriching of human society, this book is designed to challenge you and to stir you away from stagnation and the place of inactivity into fulfilling your destiny; into doing something, however small, for the betterment of society in general.

It is my prayer that for both the Christian and the unbelieving, the principles in this book will spark a change for the better.

"Can God Interrupt Your Life?" stems from a place of personal introspection, an encounter with the almighty God that left me reeling from the shock of the discovery of the self-centred nature of what I had previously thought to be a very sacrificial life! As you read this book, I pray that it leads you to find a greater purpose for your life. I pray that you may have the courage to pursue your calling and yield yourself for His use that society may benefit from the many graces God has placed in you.

Many things have influenced my thinking and the expression of my faith in my life's journey. One such thing is Alvin Slaughter's song, "That's When". My take on this song is:

"So long as you are willing to give Him what you have in your hand, the Lord can make a huge miracle of it; something that blesses the world!"

Like David, may you fulfil the purpose for which you were born, in your lifetime. I pray that history will remember you as one who was socially and spiritually relevant!!

> Acts 13:16 Now when David had served God's purpose in his own generation, he fell asleep; he was buried with his ancestors and his body decayed.

Be blessed!!
                        Can God Interrupt Your Life?

Psalm 139. 13 - 16

13 For you formed my inward parts;
you knitted me together in my mother's womb.
14 I praise you, for I am fearfully
and wonderfully made.
Wonderful are your works;
my soul knows it very well.
15 My frame was not hidden from you,
when I was being made in secret,
intricately woven in the depths of the earth.
16 Your eyes saw my unformed substance;
in your book were written, every one of them,
the days that were formed for me,
when as yet there was none of them.

Chapter 1

The Call:
Back to the original design and purpose of man

Chapter 1

The Call:
Back to the original design and purpose of man

"She would have died later anyway. That news was bound to come someday. Tomorrow, and tomorrow, and tomorrow. The days creep slowly along until the end of time. And every day that's already happened has taken fools that much closer to their deaths. Out, out, brief candle. Life is nothing more than an illusion. It's like a poor actor who struts and worries for his hour on the stage and then is never heard from again. Life is a story told by an idiot, full of noise and emotional disturbance but devoid of meaning."

William Shakespeare: Macbeth, Act 5 Scene 5

I have come to understand upon various reflective moments that it is not so important that one lived but that one lived well. This lament by Macbeth, a character in William Shakespeare's book " Macbeth", upon learning of the death of his wife and accomplice in crime Lady Macbeth, depicts a sadness at life in general. It were as if there is no meaning to life other than having been! Life to Macbeth is a tale told by a fool, devoid of meaning.

Solomon the wisest man that ever lived seemed to have come to the same sad conclusion on life when he lamented "vanity, vanity, all is vanity"(Ecclesiastics 1:2).

It is even more poignant what seems to have prompted the king to have said this:

> *Ecclesiastics 1: 12- 14*
>
> *I the Preacher have been king over Israel in Jerusalem. 13 And I applied my heart to seek and to search out by wisdom all that is done under heaven. It is an unhappy business that God has given to the children of man to be busy with. 14 I have seen everything that is done under the sun, and behold, all is vanity and a striving after wind.*

These are the words of King Solomon. A man so blessed of God with wisdom that people travelled from all over the world to see and hear him speak and administer justice. It is said that the Queen of Sheba travelled to Jerusalem to sit at Solomon's feet and sample of his wisdom and wealth of knowledge. Solomon was extremely wealthy and had according to the biblical account, 700 wives, and 300 concubines. These wives were foreign princesses, including Pharaoh's daughter and women of Moab, Ammon, Edom, Sidon, and of the Hittites. By Solomon's own words, he did everything his heart desired and spared himself nothing.

Ecclesiastics 2: 1- 11

1 I said in my heart, "Come now, I will test you with pleasure; enjoy yourself." But behold, this also was vanity. 2 I said of laughter, "It is mad," and of pleasure, "What use is it?" 3 I searched with my heart how to cheer my body with wine-my heart still guiding me with wisdom- and how to lay hold on folly, till I might see what was good for the children of man to do under heaven during the few days of their life. 4 I made great works. I built houses and planted vineyards for myself. 5 I made myself gardens and parks, and planted in them all kinds of fruit trees. 6 I made myself pools from which to water the forest of growing trees. 7 I bought male and female slaves, and had slaves who were born in my house. I had also great possessions of herds and flocks, more than any who had been before me in Jerusalem. 8 I also gathered for myself silver and gold and the treasure of kings and provinces. I got singers, both men and women, and many concubines, the delight of the sons of man. 9 So I became great and surpassed all who were before me in Jerusalem. Also my wisdom remained with me. 10 And whatever my eyes desired I did not keep from them. I kept my heart from no pleasure, for my heart found pleasure in all my toil, and this was my reward for all my toil. 11 Then I considered all that my hands had done and the toil I had expended in doing it, and behold, all was vanity and a striving after wind, and there was nothing to be gained under the sun.

To have sought to do all one's pleasure and experience all the world has to offer; to have been rich, famous, a king of Israel and yet to find life such a futile needless striving after the wind would imply that to live as it were, is not what is most important. The fact of one's existence is not the most important consideration but in that in life, others should at some point glean a benefit from your being. To live as one is meant to is the quest that everyone should endeavour to understand and fulfil.

If one would not want to live life like Macbeth's poor actor strutting his stuff upon a stage only to be forgotten upon exiting the stage of life, or if one would find more meaning in life's many adventures of the mountain (up) and valley (downs) experiences than Solomon seems to have done, then we must understand why we are here on earth. We need to have an understanding of the original design and purpose for man by his creator and the persistent call God puts out to all who have been made in his image to come fulfil destiny.

Genesis, the book of beginnings illustrates clearly the original design of God when He created man. First God made the world and everything in it that would constitute man's environment and sustenance (Genesis 1: 1 – 25). And so God provided for man, the entity He decided to create in His image, all that he will need first to live and then that which is of God Himself, necessary to fulfil the mandate for which he had been made.

> *Genesis 1:26 – 28: 26 Then God said, "Let us make man in our image, after our likeness. And let them have dominion over the fish of the sea and over the birds of the heavens and over the livestock and over all the earth and over every creeping thing that creeps on the earth." 27 So God created man in his own image, in the image of God he created him; male and female he created them. 28 And God blessed them. And God said to them, "Be fruitful and multiply and fill the earth and subdue it, and have dominion over the fish of the sea and over the birds of the heavens and over every living thing that moves on the earth."*

In the 28th verse of Genesis 1 lies the call to be more than what may become a needless unfruitful striving after the wind or a fool's tale, full of emotion but devoid of meaning. This call is the call back to the original design, to fulfil destiny, to be fruitful, and to multiply.

This is the call to exhibit the same attributes as God, the ability to establish by our word and to dominate our world, reproducing after our own kind.

Inherent in the proclaimed blessing was the ability to fulfil the mandate to be fruitful and to multiply. These abilities are many and varied, differing from person to person. In one is given a grace to be a help, in another to lead, teach, speak, and direct. Yet in others is a grace to depict by acting a message for others to emotively respond to. Some possess the ability to protect, enforce order, and to nurture, mentoring others to realise their full potential. As many and variant as humans are so are the abilities deposited in us. Your skill of oratory or your penchant to be outraged at the sight or smell of injustice is not an accident. It is intriguing how no two persons are exactly the same, even identical twins!

Often times the unveiling of the graces and abilities deposited in us by God to aid us in our calling dawns on us with internal stirrings often exhibited as either great enjoyment derived in doing something or great discomfort and upset at seeing something done not quite to the standard of our internal compass. In may present as a yearning to provide something such as a service that is currently absent so that the lives of the people around you are made better by it. When you are moved repeatedly by what you see done in a substandard way around you to want to get it done better, you ought to pay attention to the trend of events because inherent in that discomfort is a key to your assignment in life.

When you do particular things with an ease that comes to you not just from the repetitiveness of practice and you derive great satisfaction in doing it well, you have stumbled most likely on to your purpose in life. For everything that God calls us to, we are given the ability or grace to do it excellently and effectively. For every assignment, there is provision made!

We find that in making the purpose for creating man known, God instructs without ambiguity; without room for misunderstanding or misinterpretation, that man ought to be fruitful and multiply. He enunciates "Be fruitful" in the same way He spoke light into being – let there BE light" (Genesis 1:3). There is no room or margin for flustering error – be fruitful, multiply, fill and subdue the earth, replenish the earth and reproduce after your own kind (entities also bearing the image and attributes of God, establishing by their word and deed the glory of God here on earth).

Often the call to be fruitful and to multiply seems to be misinterpreted to imply biological procreation only. The call to have dominion may be misappropriated for the acquisition of wealth and status, personal pursuits that do not necessarily add to society in any way. And we are often torn between serving God's purpose and pursuing personal aspirations as if the two were divergent of each other. There are the secular pursuits of a job, career, or profession and then there is my faith or relationship with God; as if the one was able to exist without the other. In my opinion, personal aspirations are worth undertaking only inasmuch as they are the tools or vehicles through which we can fulfil the God-given mandate. One is not separate from the other.

A banker is placed in the halls of a bank or financial institution to use the grace of understanding numbers, money, or finances as a tool of propagating the kingdom of God. In like fashion the bus driver, lawyer, doctor, nurse, businessman etcetera all have the avenue within their various undertakings to be fruitful and to multiply. Godly teachers are needed in schools to mold young minds to think the way of God. Declining moral standards in our society today may be indicative of someone failing to man their post, not just as a parent but as a professional, to use that opportunity of the formative years to shape the future pillars of tomorrow's society.

I strongly believe that it is time we realised that this call from God is not just a call to have children or to possess wealth. My considered view is that these proclamations have a much deeper and divine meaning than is immediately apparent to us. Procreation and wealth acquisition are but a part of what can be considered a three-pronged mandate given to man by the Lord:

> *1 Procreate in the biological sense of the word: be fruitful and multiply, fill the earth.*
>
> *2 Dominate, exercise authority over your world: fill the earth and subdue it, and have dominion over the fish of the sea and over the birds of the heavens and over every living thing that moves on the earth.*
>
> *3 Make of your same kind – in the nature of who you are in the original design: be fruitful and multiply, fill the earth.*

It is the last two of these three-pronged mandate that we seem to mostly neglect. We do well in procreating biologically. What we appear to not do so well is the call to fulfil God's purpose of establishing His authority and dominion here on earth.

We sometimes fail to ensure that all who come into contact with us are transformed into the likeness of God (in attributes and nature, not just in looks).

The reason for God bestowing His blessing on us was so we can cause transformation wherever we are. Our very lives, professions, achievements, associations, and connections, whatever laurels we accumulate are only to serve but one purpose: to effect a dramatic change in the nature, form, or appearance of the people we encounter and in our communities. In other words, we are to leave tangible, identifiable alteration in people wherever we are; we are to have a marked effect or influence on situations or on those we encounter in our communities, workplaces, and homes.

In today's society where men appear to have left off seeking after God, doing as we please in every aspect of life, you and I are called to signpost others back to God. You are called to be Heaven's ambassador on earth, securing the interests of the "home country".

> *Romans 10:14-15*
>
> *14 But how can they call on him to save them unless they believe in him? And how can they believe in him if they have never heard about him? And how can they hear about him unless someone tells them? 15 And how will anyone go and tell them without being sent?*
>
> *That is why the Scriptures say, "How beautiful are the feet of messengers who bring good news!*

This is not just about mounting platforms to preach the gospel to others but more so about the portrayal of our God in our everyday life and transactions. And so every patient entering my consulting room must somehow leave with an aroma of God lingering in their nostril. Did they come in weighed down by a new diagnosis and a poor prognosis? I am obliged, not just from professional responsibility, to ease that burden in any way I can. That is a divine obligation placed on me by my Lord. Wherever Jesus went, He did good. By the excellence of my conduct and the practice of my craft, my patient should become aware of the difference between myself and any other doctor. In my workplace, home, and society in general, I am always on- call but not just for obstetric and gynaecological emergencies. I am on- call for the kingdom of God, that every chance encounter will showcase the Lord so that others may be drawn to Him through me. God is relying on you and me to be the vehicles through whom He is made known to all mankind.

That is the call to action to be fruitful!!!

In whichever field of endeavour we find ourselves, ours is to let our light so shine that others seeing, may give glory to our Father who is in heaven.

> *Matthew 5: 13- 16*
>
> *13"You are the salt of the earth. But if the salt loses its saltiness, how can it be made salty again? It is no longer good for anything, except to be thrown out and trampled underfoot.*
> *14"You are the light of the world. A town built on a hill cannot be hidden.*
> *15 Neither do people light a lamp and put it under a bowl. Instead they put it on its stand, and it gives light to everyone in the house.*
> *16 In the same way, let your light shine before others, that they may see your good deeds and glorify your Father in heaven.*

Because God made man in His image, man held the same power as the creator to rule and dominate his world. This birthright was lost when man chose to disobey God's given command not to eat of the "fruit of the tree of knowledge of good and bad". By this disobedience, man became subject

to his environment, no longer in a position of authority and influence. God however did not leave man in this impoverished state.

> *1 John 3:8*
>
> *He who sins is of the devil, for the devil has sinned from the beginning. For this purpose the Son of God was manifested, that He might destroy the works of the devil.*

The text in 1 John 3:8b puts out clearly the reason God had for the coming of the Lord Jesus to the earth. The son of God came to redeem mankind and restore the lost authority. God sent His son Jesus, the Christ, that mankind may once again carry the true image of He who created us.

Likewise, John 3:16 – 17 states the redemptive process the Lord put in place for mankind.

> *16 "For God so loved the world, that he gave his only Son, that whoever believes in him should not perish but have eternal life.*
> *17 For God did not send his Son into the world to condemn the world, but in order that the world might be saved through him.*

In this God gave us the most precious commodity here on earth - the sanctified life, restored into relationship with Himself and once again wielding the authority given us. But that is not all there is to our salvation.

You and I have been saved to also show forth His glory through our lives; to showcase the Lord that through our lives others may be drawn into Him.

> *1Peter 2: 9 -10 But you are a chosen people, a royal priesthood, a holy nation, God's special possession, that you may declare the praises of him who called you out of darkness into his wonderful light.*
>
> *10 Once you were not a people, but now you are the people of God; once you had not received mercy, but now you have received mercy.*

This has broader reaching implications than just speaking about the Lord to others. To declare His praise is also to make the Lord known through the excellence of our living, standing out in a morally bankrupt world by adhering to godly principles. To declare God's praise is to exhibit excellence in what we do, producing the highest quality of results at work, in whatever enterprise we are engaged in. Showing forth His praise for me is ensuring that my patients can leave a consultation knowing I have gone over and above the call of duty to bring a solution to their problem.

We must understand that man is saved for one other reason in addition to the restoration to fellowship with God: that is to help bring others to the same fate, relationship with the most high. To show forth the praise of He who translated us from the kingdom of darkness into His marvellous light is to go back to the original design, becoming the expressed image of the most high God. It is to show the excellence of God in every aspect of our lives. To show forth the praise of the Lord is to be fruitful and to multiply after our kind (the God kind).

Worryingly, the 21st century Christian would seem to be a shopper for self-fulfilment and there is one very common phrase punctuating our every conversation with God. That phrase is "Lord give me……". Whenever we go to Him in prayer it is to ask for something. Lord give me:

A good job!

Money – touch my finances oh Lord!!

A husband/wife!

A place in college/university etcetera.

And at the end of that long list of "Lord give me", we ask for grace for we must appear to care for that which is of priority to our Lord and so we pray "Lord give me grace".
Lord give me the grace to:

*Live for you

*Tell others about you. And so on.

And that is quite normal. Common sense will seem to support the notion that after all life is what you make it. Success in life

is about planning and prioritising. We are taught to structure our lives based on goals and establish a routine. Adages in our society reinforce this very notion– if you fail to plan then you plan to fail; make hay whilst the sun shines. We are constantly busy with something – school, business, chosen career path etcetera and there is nothing wrong with that.
In fact, there is everything right with that. If you have nothing doing, the bible does forbid you to eat!

> *2 Thessalonians 3: 9-11*
>
> *8 nor did we eat anyone's bread without paying for it, but with toil and labour we worked night and day, that we might not be a burden to any of you. 9 It was not because we do not have that right, but to give you in ourselves an example to imitate. 10 For even when we were with you, we would give you this command: If anyone is not willing to work, let him not eat. 11 For we hear that some among you walk in idleness, not busy at work, but busybodies.*

This bible passage will suggest that not only are we to work for our support and sustenance but we must work hard. Jesus himself was constantly hard at work. He utilised every opportunity He had to do the work for which the Father sent Him.

> *John 9:4 While it is daytime, we must do the work of Him who sent Me. Night is coming, when no one can work. 5 While I am in the world, I am the light of the world."...*

And so work we must!!

But sometimes in our lives, when we least expect it, God has a tendency to show up and interrupt what we're doing. The Lord in His divine wisdom engages our attention toward the original design - His plan for our lives. He breaks into the smoothly synced rhythm of our existence as if to say there is more to your life than this! You may already have your hands full of activity but I have so much more that I can do with you and make of your life, He seems to say. It may seem incongruous to us at the time, especially when in our private opinions, our lives already hold meaning. To have the Lord knock on our doors and seek to reset us to His original plan may seem too much of a stretch.

Oftentimes, the motive for the numerous undertakings in our lives may be what needs resetting. God's call at this point then becomes a reminder of what our focus ought to be. Remember that, that career or undertaking which you have to hand is very often the very vehicle God has given you to portray Him to the world. At other times, God's call is a complete turn away from what we are doing in the present to completely set us on a different path. In whichever format the Lord calls for our attention, understanding purpose is key to be able to yield to the master's call. To further illustrate the gap that can exist between one's call or purpose and the current reality of one's life, let us look at the ultimate example for our lives, Jesus.

Jesus came to the earth to redeem mankind back to the Father. That was the purpose of His incarnation even before the foundations of the earth were laid. Yet for 29years He lived here on earth as the son of man; Joseph His "earthly father" sharpening in Him skills of carpentry and He being obedient and subject to the instructions of Joseph and His mother Mary. At the age of 30years, He first steps up to His calling

– the lamb of God purposed to be slain for the redemption of mankind. He steps up as God's messiah and Christ, slain from before the foundations of the earth were laid. In truth, although He was the messiah from His birth, Jesus only began His earthly ministry at age 30yrs, culminating three years later in His ultimate sacrifice on the cross.

In like fashion we may be engaged in activities and endeavours that can feed into our call but that may not necessarily be the call. I believe all this while, Jesus' life was being a blessing to those in His community although He did not have a public ministry. God is asking that we come back to the original design for our lives, the mandate to be fruitful and to multiply. He has been asking in the dreams He gives us and in the encounters and promptings He brings our way. It is time that we hearkened to that call.

One of my favourite songs of all time is Reuben Morgan's piece "This is my desire". The lyrics are about giving God the entirety of oneself. In the liner notes of "God is in the House", Morgan said of this song: "The heart of GOD is for us to be completely sold out to HIM. Our thoughts, passions, and dreams (everything that makes us who we are) only have true life as they become HIS to shape and to mould. As we give our heart and our soul to GOD we then walk in the endless riches that are found in intimacy with HIM."

[http://www.lillyofthevalleyva.com/worshipmusic-thisismydesire.htm]

In my opinion, to give one's heart and soul to the Lord is to say "yes Lord" to His every bidding and call. Whatever you have to hand now, the Lord can use it as a channel of blessing to society so long as you are willing to open it up to His influence and direction. It is time, child of God, that you took up your position in your assigned place, an ambassador for Christ, showing forth His glory and reproducing of your kind upon the surface of the earth.

An ambassador always represents the "home" (where they are from) country's interests in the "host" country where they have been sent to. That is to say, the British Ambassador to Ghana is in Ghana to ensure that, British values and principles are represented in the dealings between the two countries. The ambassador does not pursue their own agenda. More importantly, they are careful not to put the "home" country's reputation in jeopardy. You as a child of God carries the same responsibility for the kingdom of God. The mandate to be fruitful and to multiply has been given to all. It takes those who are ready and willing, yielded to the master's will, and in tune with His spirit to fulfil the call of destiny. So step up to the plate!!

All of creation eagerly awaits your answer to the master's call, your manifestation as the child of God.

Prayer:

Lord stand me on the rock (Jesus) where engaged in your business, I can behold your glory!

> *Exodus 33: 21 -22*
> *Then the LORD said, "There is a place near me where you may stand on a rock. 22When my glory passes by, I will put you in a cleft in the rock and cover you with my hand until I have passed by.*

I choose to answer your call today, to fulfil your desire according to your original design for my life. Help me identify my assigned place in you and may I never vacate my post. Lord as you make clear my assignment, as you make clear my sphere of influence, grant unction for effective function.

NOTES

Chapter 2:

Can God Interrupt Your Life?

Chapter 2:

Can God Interrupt Your Life?

As a young woman, I had always been acutely aware of the nature and identity of the man I would prefer as a suitor. As a Christian woman, I subconsciously knew that this choice was not ultimately my own as I should surrender my will to Christ to lead me in this quest. This did not stop me daydreaming though. I envisaged myself the wife of a tall, broad-shouldered, and pink -lipped gentleman. Not only was he going to be handsome but he would also be full of the Spirit. Indeed it was both an exciting and daunting time of my life. Not knowing what to expect, I was earnestly trusting the Lord to bring me a man after His own heart and yet somehow afraid that He might put in my way, a man not quite like what I would rather have. I found my faith and submission to the Lord at times at variance with my desires as I sought to both please God and have my own way on the issue of marriage.

This period of my life did come to an end when almost fourteen years ago, a gentleman by the name Ernest Kwame Duah, proposed to marry me. Ironically, Ernest is neither tall nor pink -lipped. I will describe him as a man full of desire to serve his God in every way possible. We had various discussions over time, getting to know each other whilst praying to decide if we were suitable for each other. One of the questions he asked me during our initial interactions was how I felt about marrying a man whose heart desire was to serve God. I wholeheartedly answered that would be the kind of man I would wish to marry. I am after all a Christian woman. It seemed odd that I would want to do anything other than letting my husband serve the Lord. Then he asked further how I would feel if this said man, went into full-time ministry.

I suppose with hindsight it is easy to see now that he was giving me fair warning of what God had revealed to him in the place of prayer. However, I did not fully read into this question and answered unhesitatingly, without quite counting the cost, that the privilege will be mine for my husband to serve his God in the way God chose. Full-time ministry or otherwise, I was not going to impede my husband when it came to his relationship with the Father. Adam was given a wife by God as he went about the business God had entrusted into his hands. When Eve came on the scene she was not a hindrance but "an help meet" for Adam. I was going to be the absolute "Eve" to my Adam!

As God will have it, we loved each other and felt suited. We enjoyed doing similar things and I found myself falling more in love with him the more I saw him engaged in the work of the Lord, an active member of the music and youth ministries. I had found my Adam and so we got married!! Two years into the marriage, things began to unfold that now made the question I had answered without pause begin to haunt me. My husband, a brother (not in any lay leadership role), is made an elder of the church without first serving as a deacon. It happened, with no prior notice, one Sunday morning as we worshipped at the local church. As he was ordained that morning, it suddenly dawned in my spirit what Ernest had meant by the latter question. He had been assured by my answer that he was yoking himself to a woman who would support him should he be called into full-time ministry in the church. That had seemed a very far off event even if it ever became a reality. This was something that might likely happen in the far future, not anytime soon; at least not by my reckoning. And so I answered the Lord truthfully in my heart "I am not ready, Lord".

I have character flaws I need to work on. I lack tact, do not suffer fools gladly, and tend not to mince my words. By virtue of my choleric temperament, I will inadvertently bruise many an ego, heart, and spirit. I am just not a shepherd at heart. How do you partner me to a man you intended to shepherd your people when you know I am the least suitable in the sample space available to him? I am a private person, believe it or not – I can neither share my time nor space and most definitely not my husband with others. I am immensely busy in my chosen career field in medicine.

Practice in Obstetrics and Gynaecology is not only intense clinically but also physically draining. Running to emergencies is commonplace. This is the only specialty in medicine where two lives are concurrently at stake at any given time "T". Exhaustion after an on-call is a given; try gauging your energy levels after a thirteen and half hour on-call. All day, I would have been thinking, synthesising a diagnosis, implementing management plans, running, operating, and delivering babies in distress by forceps or ventouse instruments. Lord do you not care about me burning out? Am I not doing enough already? I am already sacrificing myself, putting my talents and skills as a doctor to the use of my patients whilst serving in various given roles in the church: Deaconess, praise and worship leader, committed to youth mentoring, an actively contributing member of various committees etcetera. What more can I offer?

In actual fact, what can I offer Lord, when I need so much myself!! How would I manage my career as a medic with being a Pastor's wife? Also, there is the added issue of never being able to put down deep roots anywhere with the transfer from one station to another and the implications that would have for my career progression.

These and many other somewhat valid reasons (very valid to me at least) why I could not be diverted from my set path, raced through my mind, and filled my prayer times. And so began a seven-year journey of actively pleading exemption in the place of prayer, from a task that I had not even yet been assigned to by any man. In my spirit, I sensed what was to come and I already felt overwhelmed. I hoped God would find someone else; I prayed He would and hoped I would not be found an oath breaker. I had no intention of having my life interrupted. Things were fine just as they were. I was already doing enough!

Did God let off? Not at all. His patience with me over the course of seven years will teach me that if I could not accept myself, He does accept me just as I am. His strength is made perfect in my weakness. God could have found someone else more qualified than I and much more favourably inclined to do His bidding. Yet He gently encouraged me and rebutted my arguments until one day He asked me (almost like one exasperated with a stubborn unyielding foolish child): Grace, can I interrupt your life?

In seven years, He patiently walked me through my many barriers and arguments and when the time came that my husband was invited to ministerial interview, I found myself praying that God's will may be done. First God took me through a job change three times between 2008 to 2015, taking me to Newport in South Wales, then to Surrey, and finally to Kent. Somehow, God taught me in the process that being moved from place to place in short periods for ministry-related postings was within human survival capabilities. He taught me adaptive strategies so that I moved from the not so sociable individual I was, to one who now integrated more easily into new communities. He opened my eyes to begin to desire to do more for others as I saw the impact of small things: how a smile, a handshake, a pat on the back, or a listening ear affected the lives of the people I encountered. These were not big things to do yet had big effects.

The multiplicity of contact then became a wider niche for influence for me. My medical knowledge became more accessible to people so that no longer was I a blessing just to people I encountered in the hospital consulting room, operating theatre, labour ward, or on ward rounds. I also became a blessing to the people in the small community churches where I had the opportunity to share my knowledge and expertise. It became easier over time to give my contact details out so that people could ask private questions of me following these programs. It seemed my fear of people's intrusion into my life was gradually fading away. My heart changed as did my focus for being. I discovered there was a multiplicity of avenues for impact and that has become a great joy.

Has it been an easy journey? Not at all. The Lord has had to teach me the juggling act of the life of a career woman, pastor's wife, and mother (and not just to my two biological children). And each day fresh grace is made available.

Perhaps God has been trying to refocus your attention. He may have tried to reset your motive for doing what it is you do so that it lines up with the reason He placed you in your current position in life. Perhaps there have been instances in your life where God has sought to interrupt the flow of your life completely, disrupting marriage, family, and career plans. He may have chosen to uproot you and place you in unfamiliar grounds, completely outside of your comfort zone. That can often leave us afraid and feeling over-exposed. Often, our desire to do the Father's will is held in check by the practicality of what it will entail and the fear of the unknown. However, our fears do not need to remain a stumbling block forever. When the Lord chooses to interrupt your life, He also makes available the needed resource and grace for your assignment.

Abraham, the father of unflinching faith, is a great example of how God prepares you for the interruption that catapults you to fulfilling destiny.

Genesis 12: 1-8 tells the unfolding of an unprecedented interruption of a man's life by God, taking him from all he knew and held dear and subsequently planting him in a land so alien to him. In the process, God made him a source of great blessing to generations yet to come.

> *1 Now the LORD said to Abram, "Go from your country and your kindred and your father's house to the land that I will show you.*
> *2 And I will make of you a great nation, and I will bless you and make your name great, so that you will be a blessing.*

> *3 I will bless those who bless you, and him who dishonours you I will curse, and in you all the families of the earth shall be blessed."*
> *4 So Abram went, as the LORD had told him, and Lot went with him. Abram was seventy-five years old when he departed from Haran.*
> *5 And Abram took Sarai his wife, and Lot his brother's son, and all their possessions that they had gathered, and the people that they had acquired in Haran, and they set out to go to the land of Canaan. When they came to the land of Canaan,*
> *6 Abram passed through the land to the place at Shechem, to the oak of Moreh. At that time the Canaanites were in the land.*
> *7 Then the LORD appeared to Abram and said, "To your offspring I will give this land." So he built there an altar to the LORD, who had appeared to him.*
> *8 From there he moved to the hill country on the east of Bethel and pitched his tent, with Bethel on the west and Ai on the east. And there he built an altar to the LORD and called upon the name of the LORD.*

There are some very interesting and pertinent things to note in this unfolding story. The first is that before God called him, Abram was nothing, a nobody. We know very little of Abram (meaning exalted father), who became Abraham (the father of a multitude of nations) before Genesis 12. All we know is that he is one of the three sons of Terah – Abram, Haran, and Nahor and that he had a wife Sarai (his half-sister) who was unable to bear him children. But in Genesis 12, God notices Abram and chooses to single him out for His attention. God evaluates Abram and deems him someone who would not mind having his life interrupted by his Sovereign Lord. And so one day God just asked Abram to go!

At the ripe age of 75yrs, Abram was given no destination – he was to get out from his country, from his father's house and from among his kindred and go! He is asked to go without a compass in hand, a reference point of where to head to except the assurance that God will lead him. Abram, go "to the land that I will show you". I will be your sure guide because I know where I want to take you. Your willingness to step out in faith should be matched by your total reliance on my direction to get you to that destination which only I know.

My word to you in Jeremiah 29:11 is the assurance that it will be the right destination if I lead you.

> *For I know the plans I have for you, declares the LORD, plans for welfare and not for evil, to give you a future and a hope. (Jeremiah 29:11)*

When one receives the instruction to "come", it might be an easy enough command to follow for more often than not there is a destination in sight. There often is a specific place that one's journey will terminate. It would suggest that there is someone at a specific place asking you to come to them. The route of your journey is thus simple – to travel from where you are to where that person is. To be told to go is a different matter. In which direction do I head and when do I judge that I have arrived at the destination. This calls for uncommon faith. To be told to go, with no fixed destination given, away from everything one holds dear and is familiar with, will for most of us be an untenable position to be put in. But we need to understand that it is not just anyone that God chooses to do

His bidding. It is a great privilege, though it may not feel like it at the time, for His searchlight to land on you and for Him to call you out.

God knew Abram and could trust that he will go as instructed! Can God have such an assurance in you? Can He interrupt your life and trust that you will do just as you have been asked? Or will it be a torrent of logical explanations of why the interruption is bothersome? What does it mean when the Lord interrupts a life? Let me attempt to put a scope to the diverse ways in which our lives can be interrupted by God.

To Interrupt (verb) may be defined, according to the Webster dictionary, as a move by one to stop the continuous progress of (an activity or process). Other expressions of an interruption are to cut in (on), break in (on), barge in (on), intrude (on), interfere (with), and intervene (in). An interruption could invariably result in the suspension of, adjournment of, discontinuation of, the breaking off of, a hold up of, or a delay of one's activity. It is a logical conclusion to expect an interruption to result in the laying aside of, leaving off of, the postponement of or putting back of a current pursuit, deferring or shelving of that which one is currently engaged in so that the " interrupter" may then introduce his agenda.

How do you feel about it – Can God interrupt Your Life? Can He put a stop to (bring to a halt, bring to a standstill, cease, bring to an end, bring to a close, cancel, sever, dissolve, terminate) what you find so important to you at the present? Can he pause you in your current pursuits and reset your path?

> *Psalm 115:3*
> *Now we know He's sovereign in all things and is "in His heavens and does what He pleases" { other translations: cBut our God is in heaven; He does whatever He pleases.}*

It is well within the power of the creator to say to the created "thus shall you be and so shall you do". The Lord is sovereign and does whatever He pleases. Yet in the matter of interrupting your life He seeks your consent – and His question to you today is: "can I interrupt your life?" Perhaps not so much as in the giving up of your current day job to go into full-time ministry but an increased awareness of the ambassadorial role you play for the kingdom of God. In this, the needs of the kingdom and the propagation of its principles are at the very centre of every decision and action you take. It places your life's focus as no longer the pursuit of what you will but what He wills. You must needs have an increased awareness that you belong to Him who created you and your life should therefore be willingly dedicated to Him.

When God chooses to interrupt our lives, we always have a choice. We can choose to accept His interruption and all that goes with it. Or, we can choose to reject His interruption and walk away. "Thanks for the offer God, but I think I'll pass this time. Check back with me later."

I'm a young man/woman with my whole life ahead of me. I've got plans!!
The task you demand me to attend to can surely wait a while!!
OR – this is plain impossible Lord!!

God never forces His will on anyone. He offers us the opportunity to step out in faith and the choice to obey and accept to do as He asks or to reject it and walk away. That choice is always in our own hands. It's our call, our decision. The primary question remains: Can God Interrupt Your Life?

God is always looking for the model "church" – that individual whose body is truly the temple of the spirit of God and who seeks to do His every bidding. The model church in his/her response to the master's interruption is as seen in the Church in Thessalonica (1Thessalonians 1). The Thessalonian church was an exemplary church. That church was a church full of Christian maturity.

Their maturity was shown in their willingness to have God set aside what they had to hand and refocus their attention on what He wants them to do.

> *1 Thessalonians 1: 2- 10*
>
> *2 We give thanks to God always for all of you, constantly mentioning you in our prayers,*
> *3 remembering before our God and Father your work of faith and labour of love and steadfastness of hope in our Lord Jesus Christ.*
> *4 For we know, brothers loved by God, that he has chosen you,*
> *5 because our gospel came to you not only in word, but also in power and in the Holy Spirit and with full conviction. You know what kind of men we proved to be among you for your sake.*

> *6 And you became imitators of us and of the Lord, for you received the word in much affliction, with the joy of the Holy Spirit,*
> *7 so that you became an example to all the believers in Macedonia and in Achaia. 8 For not only has the word of the Lord sounded forth from you in Macedonia and Achaia, but your faith in God has gone forth everywhere, so that we need not say anything.*
> *9 For they themselves report concerning us the kind of reception we had among you, and how you turned to God from idols to serve the living and true God,*
> *10 and to wait for his Son from heaven, whom he raised from the dead, Jesus who delivers us from the wrath to come.*

The Thessalonian church was made up of people who before hearing the gospel, were idol worshippers, engaged in various activities that served their own interests. Once they heard the gospel, these people gave up their idol worship and turned from their self -serving pursuits, to become an example to others. The became conduits through whom the gospel sounded out with others coming to the Lord on account of their example.

In our lives, every pursuit, other than that which brings glory to God and showcases Him to other people is idol worship. When I make money, progress in life, climb the corporate ladder etcetera, the intent should be to help others and to support the spread of the gospel. Any accolades and achievements one chalks up in life are of little relevance if it does not lead to the accomplishment of the original assignment- to be fruitful and to multiply (to make after the God kind).

The Thessalonian church was a church full of workers and labourers, people, who worked in faith and laboured in love. To work implies the application of thought, time, and effort. Let me draw on a little scientific knowledge to elaborate on what the Thessalonian church was called to do, the same call which has been extended to you and me.

In physics, "work" is done when a force, applied to an object, moves the object in the same direction as the force; expressed as $W = f \times d$ (work equals force multiplied by distance). Distance typically measured in meters, may be seen as a measure of the degree of influence needed to be accomplished in a set goal. It informs the magnitude of the force needful to apply in order to achieve work. "Force", a measure of the mass of an object times its change in motion or acceleration ($F = m \times a$) can be likened to the degree of effort needed for a particular task or assignment on account of its magnitude (mass) and envisaged effect(acceleration). If we apply this law of physics to human life and the impact it ought to make, we can say that the greater the assignment to hand, the greater the work needed. Hence, the applied effort, degree of applied time, and the consistency of effort will always be informed by the magnitude of the assignment. It may thus only take a little of your time and effort to accomplish an assignment. Alternatively, it may require all of your attention. When God chooses to interrupt your life, what He demands of you is directly proportional to the impact of your assignment. Jesus's assignment required the ultimate sacrifice- His life! His assignment was the redemption of the whole world. If God can interrupt your life then He will make known to you the extent of the demand to be placed on you.

To make after the God kind requires labouring: practical work, especially when it involves hard physical effort. It requires investment in the lives of others, a life of sacrifice for the benefit of others. It may not entirely fit into your lifestyle or agenda now but the child of God who is willing to have God interrupt their life must be prepared to work and labour for the good of others. There is nothing closer to the master's heart. Make the progress of God's work a priority!!! It is not enough to think about it and desire to do it. You must physically be up and doing – whether by prayer or evangelising or even by just showing love. We are required to become all things to all people that by all means, we may win some to the love of Christ. It might imply the use not just of your time and talents but also of your resources.

The Bible admonishes us to love the Lord our God with all our mind, heart, or soul and with all our strength (Deuteronomy 6:5; Mathew 22:37; Luke 10:27).

To love the Lord with all your mind would imply deliberate thought: what can I do for the Lord? What can I do for His church? What can I do for others? To love Him with all your heart will imply the involvement of every fibre of your being – the essence of you, your natural capabilities, and your God-given talents.

What has strength got to do with loving? To love the Lord with all your strength or might will imply the involvement of both your physical strength and your resources. The child of God not yet yielded in their finances to Him, not easily giving of their resource to advance the kingdom of God is hardly ready for God to interrupt their lives. Where your treasure is, there your heart will be also.

We often desire for God to use us for His glory and yet are not so ready for Him to interrupt our lives. We often ask of Him: God give me the grace to speak your word and yet we resist His promptings to study the word and to share it. We fervently declare in the place of prayer "God I want to work for you" but find the expenditure of our time and resources for the good of others or church work a great inconvenience!! Are you willing to do what it takes to prove yourself useful in his vineyard? Or are you happy only to think of it and desire to do something, just to shy away from the opportunity to make good on that desire? Are you willing to do whatever it takes for the kingdom of God to expand? Or do you do that which is in the forefront only when all can see and applaud you? Invariably, whenever the Lord chooses to interrupt the trajectory of a life, it is to reset the individual to His original plan.

> *Ecclesiastes 12:13 When all has been heard, the conclusion of the matter is this: Fear God and keep His commandments, because this is the whole duty of man.*

The blessing of Abraham came at a cost to him – moving out of his comfort zone to go to a land, the location of which he had no clue. He had no indication of the state of this land. Will it support life – can he find food for himself, family, and livestock? Abraham understood the reason for his life and reverenced the God who gave him life. He gave up everything he knew in order to keep the commands of the Lord, his God. By virtue of his willingness to have God reset his focus and interrupt his life – Abram became Abraham (the father of all nations), one whom God consults on His decisions before putting them into action.

God confers with and gives Abraham a chance to negotiate for the lives of its inhabitants before the destruction of Sodom and Gomorrah.

> *Genesis 18:17-19*
>
> *The LORD said, "Shall I hide from Abraham what I am about to do,*
> *18 since Abraham will surely become a great and mighty nation, and in him all the nations of the earth will be blessed?*
> *19"For I have chosen him, so that he may command his children and his household after him to keep the way of the LORD by doing righteousness and justice, so that the LORD may bring upon Abraham what He has spoken about him."...*

I find that I daily pay the cost of accessibility to others. There are times when perhaps I would have cherished a moment of uninterrupted time to myself. There are days when I might groan inwardly thinking I am too tired for yet another phone call or visitation. But the Lord is always gracious to show me some fruit of my labours so that I find myself encouraged to carry on. He is always reminding me that in due time I will reap a crown of glory if I faint not.

Beloved, can God interrupt your life? Can He take you off your current preconceived trajectory of life and reroute you to His divine purposes? Let Him have the totality of you and see your life become a channel of His glory and blessing.
Life is better lived under the steering of the Lord.

Prayer:

> Psalm 37:4 - Delight yourself in the LORD and he will give you the desires of your heart.

Lord I accept today that your assignment is the greatest priority of my life. To serve you, to be an instrument you can use to glorify yourself is something I do not just desire but actively seek today. I know that as I yield myself for your use, what you do with my life will cause impact, transform my society, and see me also bask in your revealed glory.

Thank you for the opportunity to serve.

Chapter 3 -

My Willing Availability

Chapter 3 -

My Willing Availability

In life, we invariably favour the one who honours us. When a protégé shows reverence and appreciation for the investment a superior is making into their life, the superior is much more inclined to do more. When they show that they are willing to do anything, go anywhere, undertake any assignment in order to maintain the favour of the superior, the superior is ever more favourably inclined towards them. The same is God's way with His children. We have understood by way of God's word that we are called and not by just anyone but by Jehovah Himself. To wit, He has made every provision for us to be able to fulfil our God-given mandate to dominate the earth, exercising godly authority over it and reproduce after our very kind (the God kind).

We must understand that our being favoured and called of God has never been in question. He has given us, in addition to life, every grace and opportunity to be of use to Him. As assets in His hands, the Lord is watchful and protective of those whose lives have been laid open for His pleasure. He gives Egypt for your ransom, Cush and Seba in your stead because you are precious in His sight. He gives nations in exchange for your life

> *Isaiah 43: 3 – 4*
> *3 For I am the LORD your God, the Holy One of Israel, your Saviour. I give Egypt as your ransom, Cush and Seba in exchange for you.*

> *4 Because you are precious in my eyes, and honoured, and I love you, I give men in return for you, peoples in exchange for your life.*

What may be in question is our posture towards His assignment, that for which God has appropriated us: to possess nations and to cause transformation. The question I want you to ask yourself today is:

> *-Are you available for God's assignment (to cause transformation)?*
>
> *-And is that availability willingly given or grudgingly given?*

I want to challenge you to take the right posture before God; my prayer being that by the help of the Holy Spirit I can place in your hand a single key that grants you access to God's favour and makes you into a transformation causer.

Willingness can be defined as the state of being ready, eager, or prepared to do something. Willingness initiates promptness to respond or to act. In other words, willingness implies that one is inclined or favourably disposed in mind towards something, and in this particular instance God's assignment for your life.

Availability denotes the quality of being able to be used or obtained. It is the state of not being too busy to do something required of you. To be willingly available to God is to be open and waiting, always accepting of His interruptions if required, so that our lives can be used as conduits of blessing to our world.

A lot of times, the 21st century Christian treats God as a Santa Claus or supermarket: there to provide, there to supply, and all for my benefit. We oftentimes have the opportunity and means to possess the nations for our God but we do not. We often do not showcase our God by the excellence of our conduct and speech that others may see and approach His light, being led unto salvation. We concentrate so much on our livelihood that we forget who gave us life and the ability to enjoy it.

We often are willing to be used of God but are not available. Occasionally we are available but oh, so reluctant to be used. In our tin – focus on the reason for our existence, we often forget our mandate to reproduce after our kind (the God kind). We give an extensive set of excuses why God's agenda must take a back seat to ours. And we try to deny our identity claiming a desire to not want to earn the reputation of a "Christian fanatic" (chrife). The Holy Spirit prompts us to witness and to recruit others into the kingdom but we let the opportunity go because it's not cool!! In my opinion, it is an even more frustrating experience when we lend half our attention to the task, seemingly engaged in God's work but only half-heartedly so.

To reiterate, His grace and manifold blessings, provisions, opportunities, promotions made available to us are but to one end: to serve His purpose. And that is to demonstrate God here on earth. It is to possess the nations for our God and to make His might and glory known!! And so there are times when the God who formed you and breathed into you; the one who knew you before you became, interrupts the frenzy that is your life. There are times when He says "beloved I see you headed from point A to Z but can you trust me that my word in Jeremiah 29: 11 is for you?"

> *For I know the plans I have for you," declares the LORD, "plans to prosper you and not to harm you, plans to give you hope and a future (other versions: to bring you to an expected end.*

In this passage, the Lord is reminding us that "I carry the blueprint to your life. I formed you and numbered your days. I declared your end from the beginning" (Isaiah 46: 10)."I would rather take you from point R back to K and re-route you via point C to D. And although point D was not your intent, I knew you before you ever were and planned your days from the beginning of time. I know point D is the fulfilment of my purpose for your life".

We may not find it easy to yield ourselves completely over to the leading and direction of the Lord. If we want to walk in the favour of God and so live meaningful lives (fulfilling our God-given assignment of establishing God's kingdom here on earth with our lives reflecting His glory) then we have to welcome and seek His interruptions. We have to yield to Him wholly, where our lives are completely, not partially, under His direction open and willing. Are you willingly available to the master? Are you yielded to His will, saying: to please you, Lord, to live in your favour, I will do anything.

For your glory, I will do anything!!

To carry God's favour, to reflect His glory, to have what it takes to cause transformation, to live a generation relevant life – there is a price to pay. It may not be convenient and it may not be comfortable.

It may be life-threatening or ego and reputation shattering.

But I am yet to see anyone willingly available to the master whom God did not glorify and cause to be a sign and a wonder.

The moon always reflects the Sun's light.

I would like us to look at the lives of three individuals who were willingly available to the master and so walked in His favour and caused transformation.

Ruth:

Ruth was a young lady living among her kin in the prime of life. She married a Hebrew, Mahlon (the son of Naomi and Elimelech), and was living a happy life. A plague spread through the land of Moab killing both her husband Mallon and his elder brother Killion. Thus widowed at a very young age there seemed only a bleak outlook for her life. But the minute Ruth said to God, I am willingly available to you things began to change.

> Ruth 1: 16 – 17 - But Ruth replied, "Don't urge me to leave you or to turn back from you. Where you go I will go, and where you stay I will stay. Your people will be my people and your God my God. 1:17 Where you die I will die, and there I will be buried. May the LORD deal with me, be it ever so severely, if anything but death separates you and me."

When Ruth spoke these words, she was making a declaration of her willing availability to Jehovah God!! Ruth was saying behold Jehovah, I have served my own gods and not known your favour. I have lived life my way, on my terms, and not had any impact. Today I make myself willingly available to you. I attach myself to the covenanted people of God, Israel. I not only accept to change geographical location but I accept to even die if that is what it takes to carry your favour oh God.

You see Ruth was not swearing an oath of steadfast obedience and availability to Naomi but to Yahweh and God heard her cry. And so God begins to orchestrate her steps that His purpose may be made manifest. I can picture the Lord in deep contemplation at Ruth's saying and deciding that for your willing availability Ruth, I choose to pass the saviour through your lineage.

I can almost hear the Lord whisper to her to go to Boaz 's field to glean (Ruth 2: 2 – 3), not because there were no other fields to glean from. He says to her by aligning yourself with my cause and being willingly available to me, your steps will be ordered by me. I will occasion your meeting with Boaz (Ruth 2: 4) and cause him to look with great favour on you. So unusual will be the depth of kindness shown that you yourself will marvel at being shown such great kindness (Ruth 2: 10). You see Ruth: In Boaz's loins is a son named Obed who must father a son Jesse to in turn father David from whose line the saviour of the whole world will come. That son I will use you to birth.

Come then Ruth, since you are willingly available to me Jehovah, I place upon you such glory, that all who see you will favourably look on you. They will take it upon themselves to write your CV of praiseworthiness (Ruth 2: 5-7). All people will work toward your good (Ruth 3:1) until my purpose is served. You may not be the prettiest girl in Israel but Boaz wouldn't know what hit him for he won't rest until he has made you his wife (Ruth 3:13). For therein shall you rise into prominence in the history of men – the great great great grandmother of the saviour!!

Beloved, can I inform you that when your every desire is to serve His will and purpose you will court His favour. He will use your life for His glory. Hannah needed a son; God needed a judge and prophet. When Hannah willingly made her womb available to God (1 Sam 1: 11), she received her heart's desire for a child. It was only at the point when Hannah indicated her willingness to give back the son Jehovah God gives her to the Lord, to serve in His temple all the days of his life that God released Samuel unto her.

Ruth would have died a poor childless widow but for her willing availability to the Lord.

If you want to leave your mark on the world then you need God's favour. To obtain His favour, be willingly available to Him. What He does with your life is what will cause transformation – history will remember you!!

Abraham

In the previous chapter, I introduced the man Abraham (previously known as Abram) who was a seventy – five year (75yr) old man at the time we first hear of him in the Bible. The son of Terah, he was married to His half-sister Sarai (the daughter of his father by another woman, not his own mother).

He is an unknown quantity until Genesis 12: 1 – when suddenly Abram bursts into prominence in history because Jehovah speaks His name. God says to Abram – leave All that you know- kin, land, whatever you are doing now and go!

The Logical question would be, leave to go where?- "to a land, I will show you".

I would have probably said, Lord, I said to use me but not quite in this way. But Abraham does exactly what the Lord is asking of him – willing and available.

> *Genesis 12: 4 – So Abram went, as the LORD had told him, and Lot went with him. Abram was seventy-five years old when he departed from Haran.*

Abram left everything he knew and held dear - no questions asked. His heart, soul, and mind were willingly available to His God. And for this God honours him and his wife (who is also willingly available and supportive of her husband) with a name change – Abraham: father of many nations and Sarah: princess, a woman of high ranking, noblewoman. Sarah automatically becomes the mother of many nations – she is Abraham's wife after all.

Looking at Sarah, the wife of Abraham, let me take a short digression and address the wrong ideology of modern-day Feminism! Modern feminism has debased womanhood and marriage completely so that the word wife seems to be a derogatory term. Feminists will have us believe that the woman is the second sex when she is defined in relation to the man (woman – taken out of man) and marriage is the legalised enslavement of the woman who must be liberated forcibly if necessary; whether she wishes to be liberated or not because a woman willingly submitting to the authority of her husband is a pitiful brainwashed entity (paraphrased from Simone de Beauvoir's book: the Second Sex)

But when you read Genesis 2: 18 – 23, it is obvious from God's word that the source of the woman is indeed the man – the woman was created out of the man in response to the need of a suitable "helper" – one who is to help the assignment, not completely take it over or seek her independence for that matter.

God put order in the home for a reason: the man is the head of the woman as Christ is the head of the man and God is the head of Christ (1 Corinthians 11:3). Does God being the head of Christ make Christ inferior to God – no (John 10: 30 states "I and the Father are one") but Christ submitted himself to the will of the Father.

In the same way, the man is the head of the home, receiving the direction and assignment for the family; the suitable help (wife) being willingly available to support and meaningfully contribute towards the realisation of the vision by submitting to the God-given authority of her own husband.
There is a grace to being a wife!!

Sometimes, being a "suitable helper" of the husband's assignment may be what brings a woman to prominence e.g. Ruth, Sarah, Priscilla the wife of Aquila.

Many a professional woman has a problem with biblical womanhood.

But note: All you are and achieve is to aid your being a suitable helper of the man's assignment. A woman who truly is willingly available to the Lord is submitted to the Lord and so easily places her strengths under control of the husband's authority (submission – strength placed under control). By all means have strengths – be well educated, well-read, industrious, commanding your own means of income streams etcetera but be Christian enough to possess your marriage for God by serving your husband's God-given assignment.

It might be better to not marry if you cannot see as God sees on the matter of wifely submission.

Sarah shoots to prominence – noblewoman, mother of many nations because of her husband Abraham's assignment. And Abraham's wealth begins because of Sarah. God causes king Abimelech to give bountifully unto Abraham for daring to desire Sarah his wife (Genesis 20: 1 – 16). Abraham's wealth is made!!

Being willingly available to the Lord places Abraham in a unique position with God. The Bible describes Abraham as GOD'S friend, one with whom God discusses His next move

> *(Genesis 18: 17 – 19) – shall I hide what I'm about to do from Abraham?*

I pray that God will call you HIS buddy– one He discusses with!!

Abraham stands in a special place – able to negotiate with God because he was first willingly available for God's purposes!! And today all nations are truly blessed because of Abraham.

Mary

Mary is a young virgin betrothed to a righteous man called Joseph. She is planning the wedding of the century – colour codes, invites, social media publicity, and so on. Then in Luke 1: 26 everything changes: God sent the angel Gabriel to the young virgin Mary.

The news that he carries is not just life-changing, interrupting her wedding plans but also life-threatening. The essence of his message is: Mary, God intends to place a pregnancy in you do you consent? The reason God has chosen to do this to you is that you have found great favour in His sight. Of all the women in this world you Mary, are the one chosen for this task – do you consent?

How would you have received this news were you to be in Mary's shoes? Mary is an unmarried virgin betrothed to Joseph and living in a theocratic society. Obedience to God and His law is at the centre of life in this society. If found to have been with a man before marriage, Mary is guilty of adultery by virtue of being betrothed. The punishment for this is stoning to death.

From ages past, the principles of God have not changed. Fornication and adultery is a sin before God now, just as it was then.

> *1 Corinthians 6: 18 – Flee from sexual immorality. Every other sin a person commits is outside the body, but the sexually immoral person sins against his own body.*

The Church family you belong to may only suspend or mete out some disciplinary action to you but the enemy (Satan) now has room to "stone you to death" if you do not repent. The guilt the enemy visits on the sinner alone can be soul-crushing. Once given the opportunity, Satan continually stands as the accuser, bringing into sharp focus past sins we would rather be rid of.

May God grant you the grace to live a life of purity for Him before and after marriage.

If Mary consents to be the vessel through whom the saviour is brought into the world, she will be guilty of adultery by the Mosaic law. What then will happen to her if upon being questioned about her pregnancy, Mary was to answer: "I have been with no one but I'm pregnant by God's favour!!"

Such sacrilege, such infamy! Do you dare to blaspheme God on top of your indecency? I bet the stone-throwing would have started without any hesitation. How would Mary prove that she spoke the truth? There had been no other person present at the annunciation. A people who held the very name Yahweh sacred will be greatly indignant at what sounds to the human mind an implausible claim. There is no indignation more potent than righteous indignation. Death by stoning will be swift and merciless.

These thoughts might have raced through Mary's mind. Mary may have mentally felt the horror that could result from this assignment. Common sense will indicate that refusal of the assignment will be a wiser course of action. But instead, we hear Mary's willing availability as she surrenders for God to do with her as He pleases.

> *Luke 1:38- "I am the Lord's servant," Mary answered. "May it be to me as you have said."*

I have never personally been so moved by any statement quite like how these words of Mary move me. The implications are beyond imagining. "My betrothed will most certainly not marry me anymore (for who would marry a loose woman) but may it be to me...."

"This is seriously inconveniencing but may it be to me...."

"I will become the gossip fodder for the community Lord. My shame will be endless but may it be to me......". "I could be killed Lord but may it be to me....". The threat of death is a risk I am willing to face for your sake Lord! I am willing. I am available! And for this, all generations have called Mary blessed, just like Mary prophesied on meeting her cousin Elizabeth, the mother of John the Baptist.

> Luke 1:46 – 48
>
> *46 And Mary said, "My soul magnifies the Lord, 47 and my spirit rejoices in God my Saviour, 48 for he has looked on the humble estate of his servant. For behold, from now on all generations will call me blessed;*

Can you imagine the power of the Spirit Mary experienced as the saviour was formed in her womb? Even at the sound of her voice Elizabeth is filled with the Spirit of God and begins to prophesy.

You see beloved, the God factor is the needed ingredient that transforms your life from the ordinary to the extraordinary. It is that which causes you to impact others and bring about transformation. It is not your accolades, degrees, money - those are but vehicles. When your life is yielded to Him, you give the Lord your all. In choosing to delight yourself in the Lord and seek Him, He makes your life glorious, an example, that He may be glorified by all.

Psalm 37: 4 – 6

> *Delight thyself also in the LORD: and he shall give thee the desires of thine heart.5 Commit thy way unto the LORD; trust also in him; and he shall bring it to pass. He will make your righteousness like the dawn and your justice like the noonday sun".*

In other words, a life yielded and available for God's use is one He Himself showcases so the world can behold His splendour! It is not always easy to let go of plans and devices and to trust solely in the grace and provisions of the Lord. Oftentimes our human understanding is to strive to achieve prominence. We, therefore, become deeply engrossed in our pursuits, so much so that we miss the many opportunities God gives us a chance to be glorified and to be impactful as He is glorified through our lives. It calls for faith to be completely yielded to the Lord; to know that He is a rewarder of those who diligently seek Him.

> *Hebrews 11:6*
> *6 But without faith it is impossible to please Him, for he who comes to God must believe that He is, and that He is a rewarder of those who diligently seek Him.*

It takes faith to lay open every aspect of our lives to the Lord. To be able to say "have your way Lord and do with me as you please" requires an immovable trust in the Lord. It requires faith in His ability to take you to an expected end. In our walk with the Lord, it is imperative that we know He is: a rewarder of all who diligently seek Him. The diligent is not just willingly available to God for His use. The diligent actively seek His interruptions. Their very lives are a committed pursuit of He who having formed them, knows the path to set them on.

All the three lives we have looked at had one thing in common - willing availability to the Lord. The opportunity to be a blessing is made available to everyone born of a woman but the effect of every individual life on society varies. Some die and the world barely notices. Others pass on and the whole world comes to a momentary standstill, in recognition of the contribution their lives made to the fabric of our society.

I learnt as a young student the quadratic equation:
"$y = ax2, bx+c$". As I have gotten older, this equation has taken on a different meaning and application for me as I have pondered how one life varies from another solely by virtue of how each individual lives. The impact on society's fabric by two lives laid side by side in comparison can be easily worked out by the degree of availability the one life has for God's manoeuvring compared to the other.

"y" may be considered as the magnitude of a person's reach or influence on society in their life span. The coefficients "a" and "b" denote natural graces or abilities and opportunities in life respectively. In life, we all have been given abilities and time (opportunity). If the constant "c" is the blessing of salvation that every child of God has in their life (Christ in your life), then the value of "y" becomes directly proportional to the value of "x": the extent to which that individual makes himself or herself available for God's use. The more available you are for the master's use, the greater the value of "x" and hence by proportion, the greater the value of "y". In other words, the degree of your impact in society is a reflection of your willing availability to God! Since salvation, ability, and time is freely given to all, there is no limiting factor to one's reach other than oneself.

We have time and opportunity but not eternity here on earth and so get doing now and do not put God off to a time in the future, a time that may not be yours.

> *Ecclesiastes 9:10- Whatever you find to do with your hands, do it with all your might, for in Sheol, where you are going, there is no work or planning or knowledge or wisdom.*

If we yearn to impact society, the time is now. There is no other guaranteed opportunity than the now to show willingness and be available for the master's use. Because for man death is a certainty and yet of an uncertain timing, we must strive to answer the master's call now, laying aside every besetting entanglement that holds us back from fulfilling our destiny.

God is looking for men and women with humble hearts; who will sacrifice everything for the cause of Christ now and who will stand in the gap as servant-leaders for their families and Christ's Church. Can God count on you? Will you willingly be a part of God's end-time army? Can God interrupt your life?

> *Psalm 110:3-*
> *Your people will offer themselves freely on the day of your power, in holy garments; from the womb of the morning, the dew of your youth will be yours.*

God has always actively sought for Himself a people to call His own. He has always been in the business of building a people of power. These are the ones who go out in the power of His Spirit, doing exploits for God and turning hearts to Him. Are you willing to be a part of this great force - taking territories for our king?

The call to "reproduce after your kind and to possess the nations" is a military battle cry – an order issued by the Lord that you and I should go into enemy territory, infiltrate and conquer. The world blatantly sets aside the precepts of God as if they chanced into life by their will power. Many false ideologies exist that drive man further away from the creator as we buy into them. Self-indulgence and gratification of the fleshly desires are at the forefront of man's desires, so far removed from God and His dictates. God is calling all His children to help reset minds and hearts to Him. This is the battle cry God has issued out. It is a call to take back territory from the enemy. The good news is that you are not doing any physical fighting.

> *Jesus said, "I will build my church and the gates of hell shall not prevail against it" (Matthew 16:18).*

That presupposes that Jesus is the one doing the battle and the battle's end result is already predetermined. All you and I have to do is to be willing to go. The end is the glory of the Lord!

Finally be willingly available in the place your God has placed you: what you are doing is the vehicle God will use. It is the reason He has placed you where you are (doctor, lawyer, hairdresser, engineer, nurse, banker, pharmacist, etcetera). You can neither carry His favour nor see His glory nor cause transformation until you are firmly standing in the place God has provided for your assignment. Whatever you have at hand to do, let it be a conduit for the propagation of God's kingdom.

You may be doing good, impacting, and bettering the lives of others and yet not have a relationship with the Lord. May I recommend a relationship with the Son, Jesus. When He comes into your life, He moves you out of the kingdom of darkness into His marvellous light. He multiplies your scope of influence for His glory. Your willing availability can only be evident when you have a relationship with the Son (He who has the Son has life- 1 John 5:12). There is no other name given by which mankind must be saved except the name Jesus.

Give Him your life and your heart and watch Him make you a sign and a wonder unto men. In your willing availability to the Lord, laying time, skill, and resources at His beck and call, He will glorify you. Mary, Ruth, and Abraham are but examples. May history take note of you as you willingly avail yourself for the Master's use.

Prayer:

Matthew 16:24

24 Then Jesus told his disciples, "If anyone would come after me, let him deny himself and take up his cross and follow me.

Lord I understand that to be generationally relevant, I must be willing and available for your use. I pray today that you will help me take up my cross and follow you. I am counting the cost and whilst daunting, I choose to see the glory of you at work in my life as the weightier matter. May you grant grace that I may be willingly available for your use.

Chapter 4 -

For such a time as this!

Chapter 4 -

For such a time as this!

I have often wondered how God orchestrates the seasons and times of our lives. If Martin Luther King had lived in this century, would he have made the profound impact on civil rights as he did in his day? Would history still be resounding the famous words of this great man, daring to have a dream of a world where skin colour was not a dividing denominator; where one's inclusion in society was a given right irrespective of race, gender, belief, age etcetera? I have oft mulled over in my mind why South Africa's Nelson Mandela, Ghana's Kwame Nkrumah, India's Mahatma Gandhi, and Ethiopia's Haile Selassie were born when they were. Was it a chance happening that Florence Nightingale (12 May 1820 – 13 August 1910), credited as the mother of nursing practice as we know it, lived and influenced society in the time she did?

I would not be able to exhaust the intrigue I have about history's greats such as Harriet Tubman and Sojourner Truth, both African Americans who sought the abolition of slavery. Harriet Tubman was well known for helping 300 fellow slaves escape slavery using the Underground Railroad and Sojourner Truth was a passionate campaigner who fought for women's rights, best known for her speech " Ain't I A Woman". Then there was Rosa Parks, whose refusal to give up her seat in a segregated bus and the subsequent fallout led to the nationwide boycott of these segregated buses. This event culminated in the freedom I have today to go wherever I want and sit not by my skin colour but by the availability of a seat!! History is littered with men and women who by their simple existence impacted society for the better. I have often wondered why they were at the time they were! Why am I here on earth at this particular time, not a generation earlier nor later? The individual who would fulfil their God-given mandate to be fruitful and to multiply, to have dominion and reproduce after the God kind, learns to ascertain the reason for their existence now. If we believe we are alive just because we are, then we fail to see God's plan in totality. We will find ourselves unfulfilled in life and more dangerously, of no benefit to our generation. An attempt to answer "the why" of my existence inevitably leads me back to the one who gave me life.

There are many schools of thought about how the earth and humankind came to be. The theory of the big bang and evolution are some of the few ways man has strived to explain his existence on earth. Contrary to this, I and many Christians all over the globe believe in the creation of the universe and man by the sovereign God. In my opinion, the story of creation set out in Genesis 1 provides a solid reason how things came to be. Further, Jeremiah 1:4- 10 sets out the purpose of God for man, an expansion of His original design in Genesis 1: 26-28 which we explored in the first chapter of this book.

> *Jeremiah 1:4- 10*
> *4 Now the word of the LORD came to me, saying,*
> *5 "Before I formed you in the womb I knew you, and before you were born I consecrated you; I appointed you a prophet to the nations."*
> *6 Then I said, "Ah, Lord GOD! Behold, I do not know how to speak, for I am only a youth."*

> *7 But the LORD said to me, "Do not say, 'I am only a youth'; for to all to whom I send you, you shall go, and whatever I command you, you shall speak.*
> *8 Do not be afraid of them, for I am with you to deliver you, declares the LORD." 9 Then the LORD put out his hand and touched my mouth. And the LORD said to me, "Behold, I have put my words in your mouth.*
> *10 See, I have set you this day over nations and over kingdoms, to pluck up and to break down, to destroy and to overthrow, to build and to plant."*

This was an interesting discourse between Jeremiah and Yahweh, the sovereign Lord. The Lord calls up Jeremiah to inform him that even before he was, God knew him. That is to say, before the fusion of gametes and the subsequent cellular divisions of the fused nuclei that progressed from zygote to morula to blastocyst, He knew him. God's plan concerning Jeremiah predated his transition from embryo to foetus. Before the dawn of that forty-week incubation that led to his birth, the Lord knew Jeremiah and had already set out his purpose in life. God had already planned that Jeremiah will be His mouthpiece to the nation Israel, the impact of that assignment spanning out across to generations yet unborn. Jeremiah's relay of what the Lord told him continues to be relevant to the present age.

Generations to come, if the Lord should tarry, will find themselves enlightened and blessed by those same words. Jeremiah had a role to play, namely to step up to the plate and fulfil his assignment.

Like Jeremiah, the Lord reaches out to you and me today, to affirm that even before we took shape. Before the beginning of time, He knew us. He numbered our days and planned an entry into the world in a time frame designed for maximal exhibition of His glory through us. What a fabulous piece of knowledge! To know that I am, not just for the sake of life but for a set purpose. To know that I am born and live in the current generation because the one who formed me numbered my days and set the course of my life. The thought detail involved in this is exhaustive: every aspect conducive to the fulfilment of my assignment is well planned out. God chose not just my being (the parents to whom I will be born) and the timeline (when I will be born). He also in His manifold wisdom, orchestrated my every experience in life to bring me to the point of great impact designed for my being. He fore planned all this when He conceived the thought of creating the world and man. I was made in every minute detail even before the existence of time!

Beloved it is no accident that you live now and do so in whichever geographical location you are. It is no accident you are who you are in the way you are.

What an exciting assurance: to know that my every step has been preordained and my purpose shall not be lost only if I can recognise it and allow God room to operate in my life. In this way, He brings to fruition now, the seed of grace planted in me from my inception. The purposes and plans for God have always been benevolent.

If you consider that the moon shines because it reflects the light of the sun, then you would appreciate the depth and width of the opportunity presented you – an opportunity to reflect God's glory in a time such as this.

Acts 17:26 (Amplified Version)

And He made from one [common origin, one source, one blood] all nations of men to settle on the face of the earth, having definitely determined [their] allotted periods of time and the fixed boundaries of their habitation (their settlements, lands, and abodes)

"For I know the plans I have for you," declares the Lord, "plans to prosper you and not to harm you, plans to give you hope and a future." (Jeremiah 29:11)

God plans to bring to pass everything He thought of concerning you the day He planned your existence. That plan is to do you good all the days of your life. The execution of that plan necessitates you living your life according to God's script. There is also a need to understand that the time is now, not some distant future, for the manifestation of what the Lord has designed for you. And believe you me it is wonderful indeed!!

1 Corinthians 2:9

But, as it is written, "What no eye has seen, nor ear heard, nor the heart of man imagined, what God has prepared for those who love him".

Your every step in life has been designed with great thought to the glorious, yet to be revealed, purpose of God for your life in mind. No eye has formed its shape, neither has any mind yet conceived its magnitude. So long as you stay the path of He who formed you, your destiny in life shall not be abrogated. The bible, being the infallible word of God, is written by the inspiration of the Holy Spirit for our learning. Let us step into the bible to look at two individuals, one in the Old Testament, the other in the New Testament, who understood the need to be up and doing in their time.

Queen Esther

The biblical story is told of a young Jewish maiden Hadassah. She was the orphaned daughter of Mordecai's uncle, another Benjamite named Abihail. Both Hadassah and her guardian found themselves as prisoners of war, taken from Israel into the Persian empire with Ahasuerus as its King. One can only imagine what little hope if any, the young maiden Hadassah would have had of acquiring prominence for herself. Not only was she a woman in a very patriarchal society but she was also a slave. Although the Masoretic Text (the authoritative Hebrew and Aramaic text of the twenty – four {24} books of Tanakh in Rabbinic Judaism) describes Hadassah as a very comely woman, she would not have thought herself a candidate to be the empress of this great kingdom by the farthest stretch of her imagination.

> *Esther 2:7 (Masoretic)*
>
> *And he brought up Hadassah, that is, Esther, his uncle's daughter: for she had neither father nor mother, and the maid was fair and beautiful; whom Mordecai, when her father and mother were dead, took for his own daughter.*

Not only was Esther fair, but she was also beautiful. Comely, gentle, nurtured by her father's nephew as if birthed from his own loins, Esther would have had good cause to hold her head high. But the beauty of face and figure hardly mean anything in the grand scale of things when you are a slave! Not only was she not of Persian noble blood but she was a Jewish slave – a status that seemed to draw hatred and loathing the way racism in our generation pushes some people to act toward others with violence. It would appear that they feel these others are of a lesser quality of "human" than they themselves are. They believe themselves to be superior!

It is reasonable to expect that as pertains to modern-day royalty, Persian kings would not have married from outside a restricted number of Persian noble families. It is unfathomable that Ahasareus, Emperor and ruler over the vast Achaemenid Empire which spread "from India even unto Ethiopia, over a hundred and seven and twenty provinces", would have sought for himself a Jewish slave as queen. Yet Hadassah found herself queen of an empire whilst a slave sojourning in a gentile kingdom. Vashti the reigning queen was deposed, when she would not come down to be "inspected" by the King's officials at a banquet. A call goes out in this vast empire for maidens to be groomed for the King to choose from. Hadassah renamed Esther, finds herself a candidate among millions yet amid the great crowd she stands out, gaining favour in the eyes of the chief eunuch.

When God has an assignment for you He grants grace. He grants you that which gives you access, opening doors you do not qualify to enter just so that His purposes will be established.

When Esther appears before the king after a yearlong grooming, Ahasareus sees a queen, not a Jewish slave girl, and marries her. It is easy to presume that Esther's looks and fetching demeanour may have been what landed her in this great position but I beg to differ. Was there none as beautiful, if not more beautiful than Esther? I believe there were thousands of comparable beauties, each alluring in their own way and yet Esther stood out!

Inherent in God's plan for each life is the path He orchestrates for each one of us. These are different yet same in that, it brings us each to that expected end He speaks of in Jeremiah 29:11. God knows the end of a matter from the beginning of it. He knew the day will come when Haman, an unscrupulous man full of unrivalled and unprovoked hatred for Mordecai, will seek to annihilate all of the Jewish exiles in the kingdom, in the selfish pursuit of power.

> *Isaiah 46: 9- 10*
>
> *9 Remember the former things, those of long ago; I am God, and there is no other; I am God, and there is none like me.10 I make known the end from the beginning, from ancient times, what is still to come. I say, 'My purpose will stand,*

It was thus only a matter of God orchestrating the events that eventually places Esther on the throne. His purpose will stand!!

Mordecai's words to Esther upon hearing of the fate of the Jews reveal the helicopter view God had over the situation long before it ever became an issue. God had put a redemptive plan in place by placing in the royal court one who could exert influence on the behalf of the Jewish people. God will save His own one way or the other.

> *Esther 4:14*
> *For if you remain silent at this time, relief and deliverance for the Jews will arise from another place, but you and your father's family will perish. And who knows but that you have come to your royal position for such a time as this?"*

If Esther had failed to see that God had placed her in the position of influence at that time so she may be the saviour of her people, then her life would have been devoid of purpose.

Through Esther's recognition of the why of her life, she averts the total annihilation of her people. Esther's understanding of why she was in the great position she occupied although she had no qualification to be, is the reason why Israel celebrates "Purim", the Feast of Lots, a joyous Jewish festival commemorating the survival of the Jews in the 5th century BCE when they were marked for death by their Persian rulers. Esther understood what it meant to be, for such a time as this! By stepping up to the plate and fulfilling her destiny, Esther's name has been secured in the annals of history. She is to this day celebrated by both Jews and non- Jews alike.

Paul (aka Saul of Tarsus)

The Apostle Paul is yet another example of one who understood the reason for his living in the time he did. He understood that life in itself on earth was but a preparatory phase of life eternally spent in the presence of God.

Paul loved God. His zeal for the things of God was unquestionable though misdirected. When Jesus revealed himself to Paul on the way to Damascus, Paul came to a better understanding of the reason for his being. In the aftermath, Paul's life, for him, was only worth living in the pursuit of Christ.

Everything he held dear in life became meaningless to him unless it served towards him knowing Christ the more.

> *Philippians 3: 4-14*
>
> *4 Though I myself have reasons for such confidence. If someone else thinks they have reasons to put confidence in the flesh, I have more:*
> *5circumcised on the eighth day, of the people of Israel, of the tribe of Benjamin, a Hebrew of Hebrews; in regard to the law, a Pharisee;*
> *6as for zeal, persecuting the church; as for righteousness based on the law, faultless.*
> *7But whatever were gains to me I now consider loss for the sake of Christ. 8What is more, I consider everything a loss because of the surpassing worth of knowing Christ Jesus my Lord, for whose sake I have lost all things. I consider them garbage, that I may gain Christ*

> 9and be found in him, not having a righteousness of my own that comes from the law, but that which is through faith in Christ—the righteousness that comes from God on the basis of faith. 10I want to know Christ—yes, to know the power of his resurrection and participation in his sufferings, becoming like him in his death,
> 11and so, somehow, attaining to the resurrection from the dead.
> 12Not that I have already obtained all this, or have already arrived at my goal, but I press on to take hold of that for which Christ Jesus took hold of me. 13Brothers and sisters, I do not consider myself yet to have taken hold of it. But one thing I do: Forgetting what is behind and straining toward what is ahead,
> 14I press on toward the goal to win the prize for which God has called me heavenward in Christ Jesus.

Paul had many reasons for which he could be proud. He was a great and renowned scholar of the law. Schooled in the Mosaic laws, he was considered an authority of these, Pharisee. He practiced what he preached and so in as far as legalistic morality goes, Paul had the moral high ground. He was of the tribe of Benjamin. This was an impeccable lineage by which one may boast, just as belonging to a great house or having contacts in high places may occasion name dropping in our times. Yet for Paul, all these became of little importance in that it no longer served the purpose for which Christ had apprehended him. If his dual Roman and Jewish citizenship were of any use to him, it was only that it served the purpose of people identifying with him and therefore giving him access to preach Christ to them.

How do you feel about your achievements in life? Do you see the link that there is between all you are and what God has mandated you to be? Do you recognise your social standing as a platform through which others might come to know the Lord? For Paul, to live was to preach the gospel entrusted into his hands when he encountered Jesus on the way to Damascus while seeking letters of authority to quash the Christian faith. He had erroneously thought the Christian faith was aberrant to the worship of Yahweh, the one true God.

The gospel he had now been entrusted with pointed to Christ, who had taken the scales off his eyes. Now he could perceive where his zeal, and strength ought to be placed.

> *Philippians 1:21 - For to me to live is Christ, and to die is gain.*

To live is Christ enabling my life and granting me every opportunity to be used of Him. To die is gain: having had the opportunity to serve the Lord in life, I can look forward to an eternity spent in His presence. And so Paul viewed life in quite a different light to the way most people do. Every second was spent in pursuit of the master's will.

His burning desire was to propagate the gospel that others may come to the saving knowledge of the Lord. Nothing else filled Paul's life with more meaning. Nothing else commanded his attention and held his commitment in the same way.

> *1Corinthians 9: 16 -17*
> *16 Yet when I preach the gospel, I have no reason to boast, because I am obligated to preach. Woe to me if I do not preach the gospel!*

> 17*If my preaching is voluntary, I have a reward. But if it is not voluntary, I am still entrusted with a responsibility....*

Paul had been entrusted with the most sacred of responsibilities – to preach Christ and him crucified. Paul's word of total commitment to his assignment is an indicator of just how seriously he took God – **"woe is me if I do not preach the gospel"**. Even in the time when I would not too willingly do, *"I am still entrusted with a responsibility".*

Even in the times when doing God's will was most inconvenient for him, Paul felt a responsibility that would not free him to do as he pleased. He felt the weight of the demand placed on his life by God. He felt at ease only when he had done what God asked of him. The fact we are Christian places a special responsibility on our shoulders – to constantly emanate God. We are not at liberty to choose when our lives will be more like Christ's. We are on-call 24/7 as far as godliness is concerned. We preach, not only by word but also by deed!

Paul understood that it was not just chance that occasioned his encounter with the Lord Jesus Christ. To have found out that he had lost time in the service of Yahweh, whom he zealously loved, in his persecution of the early church must have been particularly painful for Paul. For Paul, his every breath's purpose was to advance the kingdom of God. His complete turnaround in his pursuits is the ultimate example of a life willingly laid open to the interruptions of his maker. To wit Paul was even more energetic in his service now to God, preaching the gospel from Jerusalem through to the gentile world.

> Acts 9:20-22
> And immediately he proclaimed Jesus in the synagogues, saying, "He is the Son of God." And all who heard him were amazed and said, "Is not this the man who made havoc in Jerusalem of those who called upon this name? And has he not come here for this purpose, to bring them bound before the chief priests?" But Saul increased all the more in strength, and confounded the Jews who lived in Damascus by proving that Jesus was the Christ.

His ministry spanned from Jerusalem to Asia with stops in every major city along Roman roads. From Antioch to Cyprus then into southern Asia Minor, Paul preached. He went from Perga in Pamphylia to Antiochia in Phrygia, Tarsus to Phillipi, Ephesus, Corinth, Galatia, Macedonia, Achaea, Macedonia, Illyricum, Malta, Roman Asia, and finally Rome where he was martyred for the course of the gospel.

It is no wonder that Paul states that though the least and very last called of the apostles he achieved a Herculean task. He worked harder than everyone else. To whom much is given, much is expected.

> 1Corinthians 15: 9-10
> 9 For I am the least of the apostles and am unworthy to be called an apostle, because I persecuted the church of God. 10But by the grace of God I am what I am, and His grace to me was not in vain. No, I worked harder than all of them—yet not I, but the grace of God that was with me.

Thirteen of the twenty-seven books in the New Testament have traditionally been attributed to Paul. His exposition on the deity of Christ and his messianic assignment has formed the basis of many Protestant and orthodox theology.

Paul never lost sight of time previously lost in wrong pursuits. He believed in his given assignment for his generation and generations yet to come. From the moment Paul accepted the Lord's interruption of his course of life, there was no looking back. He was purposefully focussed, intentional in his every move, and to his dying day sold out for Christ.

> *1Cor 9:19-23*
>
> *Though I am free and belong to no one, I have made myself a slave to everyone, to win as many as possible. 20 To the Jews I became like a Jew, to win the Jews. To those under the law I became like one under the law (though I myself am not under the law), so as to win those under the law.*
> *21 To those not having the law I became like one not having the law (though I am not free from God's law but am under Christ's law), so as to win those not having the law.*
> *22 To the weak I became weak, to win the weak. I have become all things to all people so that by all possible means I might save some.*
> *23 I do all this for the sake of the gospel, that I may share in its blessings.*

Prison could not deter him, neither could shipwreck nor forty but one lashes!! I cannot see how 39 lashes will not put a downer on one's enthusiasm but not so for Paul. His life, one of sacrifice, was a complete devotion to the cause of the Lord Jesus in great exemplariness.

Interestingly both these individuals were used of God within the strengths and graces already placed in them. Esther in her graceful and comely comportment coupled with a knack for a diplomatic resolution of dicey situations. Paul was used by God in his zeal for all things pertaining to Jehovah God coupled with a detailed education in the tradition of the Pharisees, great oratory skills and logical reasoning as well as his dual citizenship of Rome and Israel. What both these two individuals needed to do was step up to the plate when called upon. They did not waste time thinking that there was time yet to come more suited for the undertaking of their assignments other than the now. We are also called to step up to the plate now, in whatever assignment God has entrusted to us; the time to act is now.

God is encouraging you and me, just as He did Gideon, to be up and doing now!! Get doing in the graces you have now, as they are!! You are called for such a time as this: recognise it and utilise every opportunity given you. Everything you need (graces, abilities, and resources) for your God-given assignment is already inlaid in you. Now step up, in this same strength, and get doing!

> *Judges 6: 14- 16*
>
> *14 The Lord turned to him and said, "Go in the strength you have and save Israel out of Midian's hand. Am I not sending you?"*
> *15 "Pardon me, my lord," Gideon replied, "but how can I save Israel? My clan is the weakest in Manasseh, and I am the least in my family."*
> *16 The Lord answered, "I will be with you, and you will strike down all the Midianites, leaving none alive."*

It may seem to you that you are lacking in many respects. Gideon knew his many shortcomings and I have felt the same too. We are however assured that God reveals Himself the most through our lives, in our weakness. When we think we do not have what it takes, He gently nudges us to just take the opportunity made available to us. As we step up for the assignment, He provides and multiplies the grace we need.

Many pursue things in life that are believed to be worthwhile but do not actually bring to fruition the purposes of God in their lives. Time spent in obtaining a good education is beneficial only inasmuch as that education enriches your life and that of others who encounter you in the course of their lives. If a mechanical engineer only ever had the scientific knowledge of his education and never once used this, he hardly qualifies for the title of engineer. Dr. Martin Luther King had grace for oratory, conveying with passion the dream he had that one day all men will be considered equal. Yet had he chosen to wait and not speak out, history would never have noted such a man ever lived. He spoke out in the time he needed to, not a month or year later.

In the same manner, the rich deposit of grace in any person's life is of nil effect if it never finds expression on the outside and in the timely manner needful for the benefit of humankind. Beloved if you understand that God called you the very day He formed you and gave you the mandate to be fruitful and to multiply, you will know that the gifting and abilities given you were so placed to help effect your calling. If you understand the essence of God's interruptions and the requisite willing availability for His use, then you will understand that you are made for such a time as this!

Now is the time to get doing. There is no time to waste. It will not be long and the master will be back. He carries with Him a reward for everyone according to their works. Would He find you to have occupied (busy working for Him) till His return? Will He find you one, who like the sons of Issachar, understood the times and knew what to do? My prayer is that illumination will birth in your spirit man; that you may understand the reason for your being and having discovered the master's will, you will step to it!

God is asking to interrupt your life and bring you to His original plan for your life at no other time but such a time as this! Some future time will not do. The time for your impact is now!!

Prayer: I give myself away:

> *Jeremiah 1: 4 – 10*
>
> *The word of the LORD came to me, saying,*
> *5"Before I formed you in the womb I knew you, before you were born I set you apart; I appointed you as a prophet to the nations."*
> *6"Alas, Sovereign LORD," I said, "I do not know how to speak; I am too young." 7But the LORD said to me, "Do not say, 'I am too young.' You must go to everyone I send you to and say whatever I command you.*
> *8Do not be afraid of them, for I am with you and will rescue you," declares the LORD.*
> *9Then the LORD reached out his hand and touched my mouth and said to me, "I have put my words in your mouth. 10See, today I appoint you over nations and kingdoms to uproot and tear down, to destroy and overthrow, to build and to plant."*

I understand that my being, at this time is not an accident. From the beginning of the foundations of the earth, you had my life completely planned out. May I not fall out of your will, purposes, and plan for me. May I be an instrument fit for your use, to be a vehicle through whom my generation will be blessed, seeing your glory through my life. Just as you taught Jeremiah and Gideon where their strengths lay, please help me uncover and appreciate the graces deposited in me. Strengthen me in my weakness and Lord, use me as you will!!

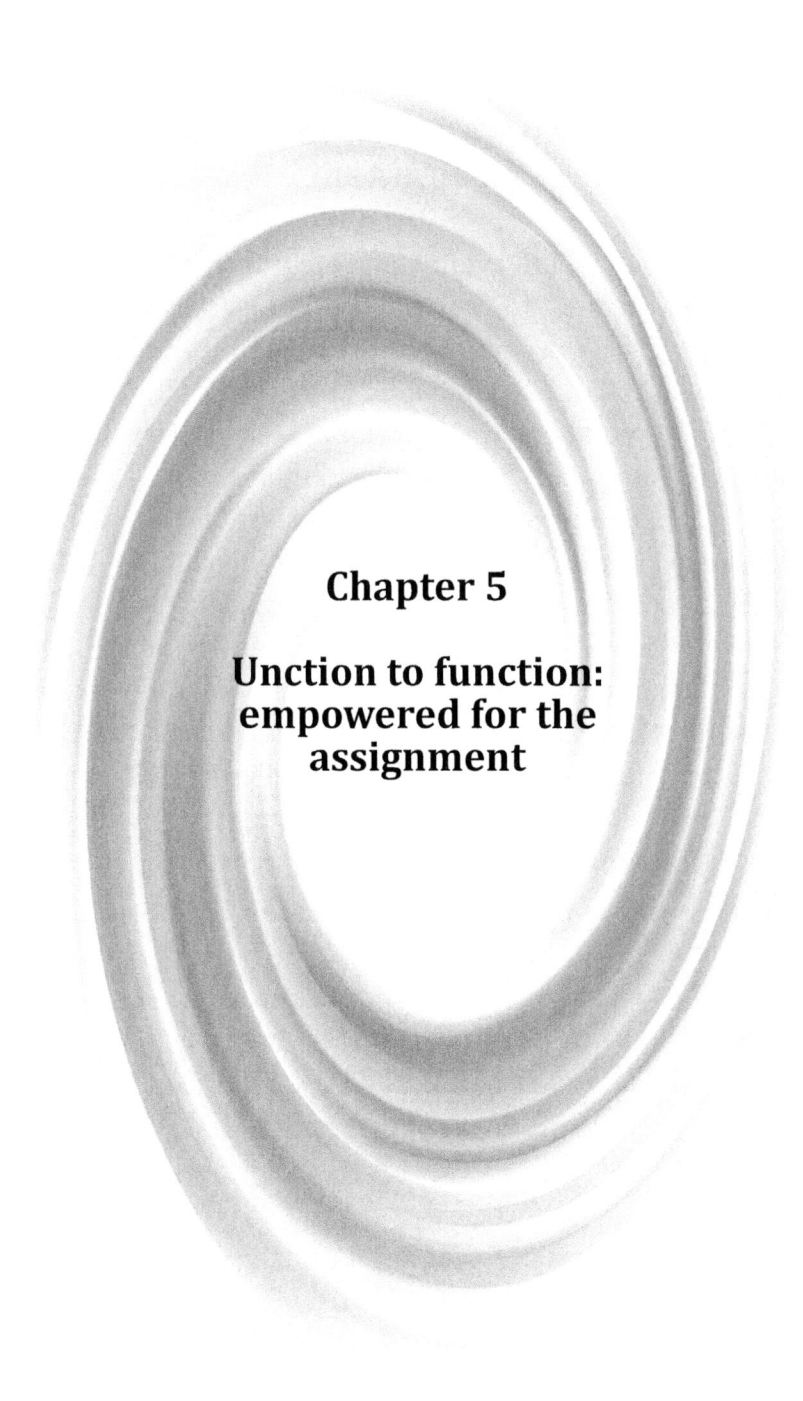

Chapter 5

Unction to function: empowered for the assignment

Chapter 5

Unction to function: empowered for the assignment

An Olympic athlete trains for a long time, in and out of season, in order to maintain the fitness levels necessary to compete at the international level. In like manner, every endeavour in life requires some preparation. Every assignment requires the acquisition of a special skill or knowledge necessary for the execution of that assignment. Medics train on average for six to seven years. They acquire knowledge of the body and how systems function. Only then are they able to detect an anomaly in function or disease. The accountant, nurse, mason, businessman, petty trader etcetera have all prepared for their respective roles. All this is aimed at ensuring that they do not fail in their assignment. And God has made the same provisions for His children, that we may be equipped for the assignment He has given us, thereby ensuring that we do not fail.

> *According to 2 Peter 1: 3-4,*
>
> *His divine power has granted to us all things that pertaining to life and godliness, through the knowledge of him who called us to his own glory and excellence.*

Yes! everything we need for a meaningful and generation relevant life has been provided for by the Lord. You and I have an assignment to undertake in life. One with far more reaching effect than anything we imagine in our general earthly pursuits in life. It is reassuring to know that we have been equipped for the task assigned to us.

We have walked through the call back to God's original design for man. We have understood that this call engenders an acceptance of God's interruption of our lives whether it be a momentary pause or a complete reset of routes and purposes. We have learnt that we must be available to be used of God: something willingly given not forced. Submission to God's will by coercion renders us unsuitable candidates for His use: only a worthy labourer may work in the Lord's vineyard. We understand also that there has never been a better time than the now to step up to the assignment and get doing.

The burning question then is: do I have what it takes for God's assignment? Herein comes the work of the Holy Spirit in the life of the believer. 2Peter 1: 3-4 gives great assurance of God's fore planning. In verse 3 of 2 Peter chapter 1, we are given a glimpse of God has put in place:

> *His divine power has granted to us all things that pertain to life and godliness, through the knowledge of him who called us to his own glory and excellence.*

In other words, the provision has already been made for whatever my life's assignment is. That provision becomes immediately accessible to me when I come to the Lord, repenting, and turning away from my sinful nature.

The power that translates from the kingdom of darkness into the kingdom of God also renews the state of man. That transformation is well attested to by the scriptures.

> *2 Corinthians 5:17-18*
>
> *17 Therefore, if anyone is in Christ, he is a new creation. The old has passed away; behold, the new has come.*
> *18 All this is from God, who through Christ reconciled us to himself and gave us the ministry of reconciliation;*

That is to say, by accepting the Lord Jesus Christ we are renewed and with the regeneration of the inner man, we are restored to the original state God made us in. We were made a people possessing the ability to be fruitful and to multiply. We carry in our DNA the ability to undertake the purpose for which we have been redeemed to Himself. That is the ministry of reconciliation. We are purposely made to draw others to the Lord. Because of that, no longer do we need to wallow in darkness trying to find out what manner of people we ought to be and how we are to achieve the tasks that have been destined for us. We just need to go back to the source of the assignment. We only need to go to the one who knew us before we ever were and ordained us for a particular destiny in life. There is provision for us to partake in the divine nature, as it were to be re- set back to who we are in the eyes of God: one created in the image of God with a mandate to dominate the earth and replenish it.

Jesus exemplified this power that the renewed man wields in every way. Everything about our Lord Jesus Christ is spectacular. Wherever He went and in whatever He did, the impact was for good, and glory was given to the father because of Him.

> Acts 10:38
>
> *38 How God anointed Jesus of Nazareth with the Holy Ghost and with power: who went about doing good, and healing all that were oppressed of the devil; for God was with him.*

What made Jesus stand out is something of God called the anointing. The anointing is the presence of the blessed Holy Spirit in a man's life that makes for effectiveness. It is not difficult to cut a tree down when the axe is sharp!! One does not need to swing repeatedly with brute strength when using a sharp instrument. However, when the instrument is dull, great physical exertion is needed to accomplish even a little. The Holy Spirit in a person's life is the "sharp edge" needed to make it possible to do God's will without sweating it out.

Jesus was able to do the father's will because he was full of the Spirit and walked in the power of the Spirit. These are two distinct things. To be filled with the Holy Spirit differs from operating in the power of the Holy Spirit. Bible tells of how after Jesus had been baptised in the Jordan, He proceeded to fast and pray in the desert mountains for forty days and forty nights, full of the Spirit.

> Luke 4:1
>
> *Jesus, full of the Holy Spirit, left the Jordan and was led by the Spirit into the wilderness, (cross-reference Matthew 4:1 and Mark1:12).*

Jesus is the express image of the Godhead and carried in Himself the fullness of the Spirit. When John baptised Him in the river Jordan, the biblical account describes the Holy Spirit descending on Him like a dove. A voice from heaven declared " this is my beloved Son, in whom I am well pleased". I believe that in that instance Jesus, the son of man, became full of the Holy Spirit, the human body being completely submitted to the steering of the Spirit of God. In addition to the fullness of the Spirit Jesus required something else of the Spirit: the power of the Spirit. The Holy Spirit led Him at once into the desert to fast and to be tempted of the devil. This was to prepare Him for the great task ahead. This preparation will lead to Jesus returning from the desert in the power of the Spirit, a fact that now translated into a ministry of the power of God to the people.

In like fashion the renewed man (renewal of the inner man occurs after accepting Jesus as saviour and Lord of one's life) is given a deposit of the same Spirit, sealing us in that newness of life. Paul explains this to the new believers in Corinth with the analogy of how one sets a seal of ownership on something purchased. The seal bears witness to all who see it that the marked item is one belonging to a particular person. Jesus purchased us back to the Father with His precious blood. The Holy Spirit has thus been set on us as a seal, making it apparent, to whom we now belong. No longer do we walk after the manner of the flesh but after the manner of the Spirit of God, by whom we cry " ABBA, Father".

> *2 Corinthians 1: 21- 22*
> *21 Now it is God who establishes both us and you in Christ. He anointed us, 22placed His seal on us, and put His Spirit in our hearts as a pledge of what is to come.*

The deposit of God's Holy Spirit in us ensures that we have an inner teacher and companion who teaches us the ways of the Father so that we can walk in the newness of life. To turn round from one's way of life to live a life that pleases the Lord will require the guidance of the Lord himself. The Spirit of the Lord opens up God to us, that perceiving, we may understand, not being like the Pharisees who though they knew of the letter of the Law, denied the power of it.

> *John 16: 12- 13*
>
> *12 I still have much to tell you, but you cannot yet bear to hear it. 13However, when the Spirit of truth comes He will guide you into all truth. For He will not speak on His own, but He will speak what He hears, and He will declare to you what is to come.*

It is the Holy Spirit who teaches us all truth. Jesus speaking to His disciples here assures them of one who will come to permanently dwell with us. He is a constant presence of the Godhead within us, teaching us how to live as children of God in all truth. He seals us for the day of Jesus's return to claim His bride (the church/ every believer in the Lord).

> *1 John 2:20*
>
> *But you have an anointing from the Holy One, and all of you know the truth.*

And so the indwelling of a man by the Spirit of God provides a constant guide in the way to walk before God and be perfect.

The ability to stand right with God emanates from God within, not from worldly wisdom gleaned with age or from experience in life.

> *1 John 2: 27*
>
> *But the anointing that you received from him abides in you, and you have no need that anyone should teach you. But as his anointing teaches you about everything, and is true, and is no lie-just as it has taught you, abide in him. (1 John 2:27, ESV)*

This same Spirit also gives an enabling power, that which was lost when sin first entered the world. This power creates room that man may be able to carry out the original plan of God – to be fruitful, multiply, and have dominion over the earth.

> *Romans 8:11 (KJV)*
>
> *But if the Spirit of him that raised up Jesus from the dead dwell in you, he that raised up Christ from the dead shall also quicken your mortal bodies by his Spirit that dwelleth in you.*

There is a power that raised Jesus from the dead. That same power in any person causes a strengthening of the inner man. The individual then becomes able to live above the base needs of the human body and overcomes the natural desire to sin. And not only that, but the individual also receives enablement to do as God instructs and in this way becomes impactful. This power is called the unction, that enabling effectiveness in the work of ministry to others.

The unction, like every gift from God, is given in increasing measure. It is not enough to have the deposit of the Spirit but one must need grow in the Spirit. The more yielded a life is to the Lord, the greater the exhibition of the unction of the Spirit upon that life. It is this "yieldedness" that facilitates the outpouring of the power of the Spirit from one's life to affect others. Jesus paints a beautiful picture of this in John 7:38.

> *John 7: 38-He that believeth on me, as the scripture hath said, out of his belly shall flow rivers of living water.*

When you are a child of God fully under the control of His Spirit, then it is from you that the effect of the power of God's spirit will emanate to affect the lives of others. Jesus was full of the Spirit. After waiting on the empowerment of the Father for His assignment, Jesus returned to Galilee now in the power of the Spirit. That power made Him stand out; the hitherto unknown Christ began to teach, heal the sick and raise the dead, doing good everywhere He went and gaining a following of hearers who quickened to return to God, at His word.

> *Luke 4: 14-15*
>
> *Jesus returned to Galilee in the power of the Spirit, and the news about Him spread throughout The surrounding region 15He taught in their synagogues and was glorified by everyone....*

You and I have one great assignment – to make disciples of the world. We are to draw others to the Lord as we have been translated from the kingdom of darkness into God's marvellous light. That assignment requires the power of the Holy Spirit, not oratory. And that is why Jesus asked the disciples to wait in Jerusalem until the Holy Spirit has come on them.

> *Acts 1:8*
>
> *But you will receive power when the Holy Spirit has come upon you; and you shall be My witnesses both in Jerusalem, and in all Judea and Samaria, and even to the remotest part of the earth."*

The power that the Holy Spirit brings, quickens and emboldens us so that we are no longer full of excuses but step forward boldly to proclaim Christ and Him crucified. It is not easy to take on the task of bringing others to Christ in your workplace, amongst family and friends without the power of the Holy Spirit enabling you. It is not easy to live a people-centered life, putting the needs of others before your own unless the Spirit of God grants you the ability. The presence of the Spirit of God at work in a life causes a transformation so beautiful it is apparent to all who behold it.

The beauty of the transformation of previously "afraid to speak disciples" to "bold proclaimers of the gospel" when the Holy Spirit came upon them, is shown in the story of Pentecost.

Acts 2: 1- 41

1 When the day of Pentecost came, they were all together in one place.
2 Suddenly a sound like the blowing of a violent wind came from heaven and filled the whole house where they were sitting.
3 They saw what seemed to be tongues of fire that separated and came to rest on each of them.
4 All of them were filled with the Holy Spirit and began to speak in other tongues a as the Spirit enabled them.
5 Now there were staying in Jerusalem God-fearing Jews from every nation under heaven.
6 When they heard this sound, a crowd came together in bewilderment, because each one heard their own language being spoken.
7 Utterly amazed, they asked: "Aren't all these who are speaking Galileans?
8 Then how is it that each of us hears them in our native language?
9 Parthians, Medes and Elamites; residents of Mesopotamia, Judea and Cappadocia, Pontus and Asia,
10 Phrygia and Pamphylia, Egypt and the parts of Libya near Cyrene; visitors from Rome
11 (both Jews and converts to Judaism); Cretans and Arabs—we hear them declaring the wonders of God in our own tongues!"
12 Amazed and perplexed, they asked one another, "What does this mean?"
13 Some, however, made fun of them and said, "They have had too much wine."

14 Then Peter stood up with the Eleven, raised his voice and addressed the crowd: "Fellow Jews and all of you who live in Jerusalem, let me explain this to you; listen carefully to what I say.
15 These people are not drunk, as you suppose. It's only nine in the morning!
16 No, this is what was spoken by the prophet Joel:
17" 'In the last days, God says, I will pour out my Spirit on all people. Your sons and daughters will prophesy, your young men will see visions, your old men will dream dreams.
18 Even on my servants, both men and women, I will pour out my Spirit in those days, and they will prophesy.
19 I will show wonders in the heavens above and signs on the earth below, blood and fire and billows of smoke.
20 The sun will be turned to darkness and the moon to blood before the coming of the great and glorious day of the Lord.
21 And everyone who calls on the name of the Lord will be saved.' c
22" Fellow Israelites, listen to this: Jesus of Nazareth was a man accredited by God to you by miracles, wonders and signs, which God did among you through him, as you yourselves know.
23 This man was handed over to you by God's deliberate plan and foreknowledge; and you, with the help of wicked men, d put him to death by nailing him to the cross.
24 But God raised him from the dead, freeing him from the agony of death, because it was impossible for death to keep its hold on him.

25 David said about him: " 'I saw the Lord always before me. Because he is at my right hand, I will not be shaken.
26 Therefore my heart is glad and my tongue rejoices; my body also will rest in hope,
27 because you will not abandon me to the realm of the dead, you will not let your holy one see decay.
28 You have made known to me the paths of life; you will fill me with joy in your presence.' e
29 "Fellow Israelites, I can tell you confidently that the patriarch David died and was buried, and his tomb is here to this day.
30 But he was a prophet and knew that God had promised him on oath that he would place one of his descendants on his throne.
31 Seeing what was to come, he spoke of the resurrection of the Messiah, that he was not abandoned to the realm of the dead, nor did his body see decay.
32 God has raised this Jesus to life, and we are all witnesses of it.
33 Exalted to the right hand of God, he has received from the Father the promised Holy Spirit and has poured out what you now see and hear.
34 For David did not ascend to heaven, and yet he said, " 'The Lord said to my Lord: "Sit at my right hand
35 until I make your enemies a footstool for your feet."
36 "Therefore let all Israel be assured of this: God has made this Jesus, whom you crucified, both Lord and Messiah."

> *37 When the people heard this, they were cut to the heart and said to Peter and the other apostles, "Brothers, what shall we do?"*
> *38 Peter replied, "Repent and be baptized, every one of you, in the name of Jesus Christ for the forgiveness of your sins. And you will receive the gift of the Holy Spirit. 39 The promise is for you and your children and for all who are far off—for all whom the Lord our God will call." 40 With many other words he warned them; and he pleaded with them, "Save yourselves from this corrupt generation."*
> *41 Those who accepted his message were baptized, and about three thousand were added to their number that day.*

What a marvel this story is! When Jesus was arrested, all the disciples run away in fear. When Peter was questioned in the inner court of Herod's palace, he was quick to deny that he ever knew Jesus.

Even when the disciples knew that Jesus was risen on the third day, they still cowered in fear of the leaders of the time and the harm that could come to them. Yet here we see something bold and beautiful unfolding. Could this man speaking really be the same Peter, a man too scared to identify himself as indeed having been with Jesus?

Could these people who gathered in the upper room, now stepping out in great boldness, be the same disciples of Christ who hid after He was crucified, jumping in fright at their own shadows?

The boldness that came from being baptised in the power of the Holy Spirit that day transformed these ordinary folk completely. They were unschooled yet spoke in different foreign languages. People from all over the world attending the festival of Pentecost could hear the gospel delivered in their native tongue. What a spectacle! What great beauty!! What an unforgettable experience.

> *Acts 17:26 (Amplified Version)*
>
> *And He made from one [common origin, one source, one blood] all nations of men to settle on the face of the earth, having definitely determined [their] allotted periods of time and the fixed boundaries of their habitation (their settlements, lands, and abodes)*

When Peter preached that day, a whopping 3000 souls were saved. It's very possible that the actual number that came to know the Lord that day may well be over 3000. Often women and children were not counted. Reading of this account in the Bible always leaves me desiring more of the Spirit. I would that my life will make even a hundredth of the impact the disciples had that day. There has never been a greater demonstration of witnessing about the Lord Jesus than that shown through these mostly unschooled individuals.

The outpouring of the Spirit makes the difference between an effective tool in the hand of the Lord and a willing but dull-edged axe that cannot be laid to the tree. Peter filled with the Holy Spirit became a conduit of God's blessing and mercy to the people of Israel so much so, that even his shadow falling on people would heal the sick.

What great transformation the coming of the Holy Spirit into a man's life brings!

The good news beloved is that the Holy Spirit has been made available to us all. When we believed, He was placed in us as a deposit, a seal of God's promise to come.

As we yield ourselves to Him, we grow in Him to the point where the Spirit acts through us to transform lives. And you do not need to be a pastor (or someone in full-time ministry work) to experience this – all you need is a heart fully yielded and obedient to the Lord.

If you consider that the body is the temple of the Lord as depicted in 1 Corinthians 3:16, then the vision that the prophet Ezekiel had in Ezekiel 47: 1- 10 takes on a new significance. It reveals to us how we already have an unction to function.

> *Corinthians 3:16 (NASB)*
> *Do you not know that you are a temple of God and that the Spirit of God dwells in you?*

Every child of God is in-dwelt by the Spirit of God. The sanctified body becomes the temple of God, where His Spirit dwells. And as one yields in greater measure to the Spirit, He begins to flow forth out of that life the way a river flows from its source.

> *Ezekiel 47: 1-10*
>
> *1 Then he brought me back to the door of the temple, and behold, water was issuing from below the threshold*

of the temple toward the east (for the temple faced east). The water was flowing down from below the south end of the threshold of the temple, south of the altar.

2 Then he brought me out by way of the north gate and led me around on the outside to the outer gate that faces toward the east; and behold, the water was trickling out on the south side.

3 Going on eastward with a measuring line in his hand, the man measured a thousand cubits, and then led me through the water, and it was ankle-deep.

4 Again he measured a thousand, and led me through the water, and it was knee-deep. Again he measured a thousand, and led me through the water, and it was waist-deep.

5 Again he measured a thousand, and it was a river that I could not pass through, for the water had risen. It was deep enough to swim in, a river that could not be passed through.

6 And he said to me, "Son of man, have you seen this?" Then he led me back to the bank of the river.

7 As I went back, I saw on the bank of the river very many trees on the one side and on the other.

8 And he said to me, "This water flows toward the eastern region and goes down into the Arabah, and enters the sea; when the water flows into the sea, the water will become fresh.

9 And wherever the river goes, every living creature that swarms will live, and there will be very many fish. For this water goes there, that the waters of the sea may become fresh;

> *so everything will live where the river goes.*
> *10 Fishermen will stand beside the sea. From Engedi to Eneglaim it will be a place for the spreading of nets. Its fish will be of very many kinds, like the fish of the Great Sea.*

We have established how upon coming to know the Lord the Holy Spirit comes to indwell us, our bodies being a temple. It is logical then to see the temple described by Ezekiel here as the individual and not a building. The particular phrase "for the temple faced east" in verse 1, stood out to me. I have come to no longer consider words and phrases in the bible as grammatical compositions meant to convey an idea or tell a story. I firmly believe every passage, word, phrase, and expression in the bible holds a meaning the Father will reveal to us if we ask of Him. As I pondered why the need to stress which direction the temple faced in this passage, it suddenly dawned on me that this was about positioning and posture.

Positioning is indicative of availability. Remember that the life willing available to the Master's use attracts His glory.

Posture is indicative of the state of the heart. A humble receptive and obedient heart is what the Lord seeks. Reflecting on the eastward facing temple brought to me an understanding that this is indicative of an individual's posture before the Lord. The Israelites generally prayed facing towards Solomon's temple wherever they found themselves in the world. This was because the temple (actual building in Jerusalem) denoted the dwelling of Yahweh. King Solomon had prayed at its dedication that when God's people prayed towards the temple, the Lord would answer. However, God now dwells on the inside of the believer which means we neither need to face towards Solomon's temple nor go into Jerusalem to pray as was the practice before the coming of Christ. We just need to enter into our prayer closet and commune with the father.

So is there a significance to the temple in Ezekiel's vision facing east? I understand this to be a posture of submission of the believer in the place of prayer to the Lord – where one is totally surrendered to Him, knowing that it is He alone who can grant the power and equipping necessary for one to become an effective tool in His hand. The temple in Ezekiel's vision was permanently eastward facing. The believer who yearns to be used of God must be permanently yielded to His Spirit. The water rose from the altar within the temple (a place of prayer and communion with the Spirit) and flowed eastward from the temple threshold (toward the world). Power does not come to us until it has been given from above. Power is not given from above until we have sought for it in prayer and fasting coupled with a total surrender to the Lord.

Remember that the more yielded a person is to the Lord, the greater the unction of the Spirit upon that life.

You cannot be empowered for the assignment to hand when the level of "yieldedness" is only ankle-deep, knee-deep, or waist-deep. At waist-deep "yieldedness", the individual is still about fifty- five percent (55%) a person of the flesh. The mind and heart are not yet fully under the Spirit's control. Sometimes by virtue of the deposit of the Spirit given at the time of believing and the partial submission to the will of the Spirit which has engendered some growth, such an individual may to most appear to be fully engaged in the Lord's business. If one is to be truly impactful, showing fruitfulness and multiplying after the God kind, then there is something of God that one needs to possess: the anointing.

The individual who desires to be used of God ought to swim in the spirit, himself/ herself completely submerged in the spirit. It is only then that the rivers of living water flow out of you to bless others. To be yielded to the Spirit is to put the flesh and its desires on the altar daily, under control. The flesh is then no longer the dominant factor but God and His precepts. Do you desire to be fruitful? Do you desire to be used for the glory of God? Then seek Him, yield to Him and receive the unction to function. That unction, needed for effectiveness, is already made available to all who believe.

All that one requires pertaining to life and to godliness is made available. The measure of unction upon a life is directly proportional to the degree of impact that life makes. Whoever shall ask will be given. Whosoever seeks will find and persistence in seeking (knock) will yield an open door to the Father.

May you receive the unction to function as you ask, seek, and knock. May He who gives in increasing measure cause streams of living water to flow out of your life and may your generation be blessed through you.

Prayer:

> *John 7: 37- 38*
>
> *On the last day of the feast, the great day, Jesus stood up and cried out, "If anyone thirsts, let him come to me and drink.*
> *38 Whoever believes in me, as the Scripture has said, 'Out of his heart will flow rivers of living water.'"*

Lord, I desire that my life may be an effective tool in your hand; one you use to glorify yourself and make a blessing unto others.

I seek a place in you whereby my actions, words, successes chalked etcetera will bring glory to you and bless my generation. I ask today for that which makes the difference: that unction divine from the Holy Spirit.

May you completely take over my life that out of me will come a refreshing for this dying world.

NOTES

Chapter 6

The blessing of the fulfilled life

Chapter 6

The blessing of the fulfilled life

The quest for fulfilment in life is the holy grail for so many individuals in this generation. With modernism has come a materialistic and self-obsessed view of what it means to live well. This is so much so that we are constantly in pursuit of something more elusive than that which King Arthur sought. Many people question why despite great successes chalked in life they do not feel fulfilled. Often there is a wide difference between what many consider as needful for fulfilment in life and the actuality of what that achievement or acquisition brings to their life.

In a society that is wholly hedonistic, where the pursuit of pleasure and self-gratification is a greater consideration than any other, it is often surprising how hollow life is felt to be. A point in question is the celebrity or affluent committing suicide, citing a lack of meaning in life. How then does the world view fulfilment? What do we mean when we say our lives are fulfilled.

Unfortunately, the world's perception of fulfilment lies at variance with what true fulfilment is. The Cambridge dictionary defines being fulfilled as "feeling happy because you are getting what you want from life: Now that I have my dream job, for the first time in my life I feel really fulfilled".

That unfortunately reveals a synergy with the self-serving leaning of the modern-day person. So long as it makes me happy, there are no other considerations to take into account.

Other dictionaries collectively put a definition for being fulfilled as being

> "satisfied or happy as a result of fully developing one's abilities or character." Being fulfilled is a process through failures and victories, rather than focused on one specific moment. A fulfilling life comes from building habits that lead to joy".

That perspective is somehow not wholly true.

The Oxford dictionary is no different in that it defines "fulfilled" as being satisfied or happy because of fully developing one's abilities or character. Almost every attempt to dissect what fulfilment is points at the individual focus with a total disregard for others.

Perhaps the Webster dictionary definition comes the closest to what the real thing is, lacking only in the context for fulfilment but hitting the nail on the head in terms of the constituents of fulfilment. It defines fulfilment as

> "feeling happiness and satisfaction, feeling that one's abilities and talents are being fully used". E.g. ... giving truly did make him feel happy and fulfilled".

In the example cited, what seems to bring about satisfaction is giving, utilising one's ability and talents fully. The context is the God-given assignment for the individual.

Many twenty-first-century Christians, unfortunately, express values similar to those of the world. We look to people, things, and places for satisfaction. We thus suffer the same hollow existence of frustrating chasing after the wind that the world does. Many of us lack joy, excitement, and satisfaction with what we have at hand to do. We often feel stuck or caught in a rut. We grind through the tedium of work and acquisition, things that in no way provide a resolution of the deep yearning we have for something more. Many lack direction and clarity of purpose. It was as if we do because we must.

This obvious lack of satisfaction and fulfilment in life is because by choice we mostly live in disobedience to God. If you consider that man has a mandate to fulfil from the time of birth to the time of death, then the fulfilled life can be described as the life lived according to the original plan for man.

> *Genesis 1: 26 -28*
> *26 Then God said, "Let us make man in our image, after our likeness. And let them have dominion over the fish of the sea and over the birds of the heavens and over the livestock and over all the earth and over every creeping thing that creeps on the earth.*
> *27 So God created man in his own image, in the image of God he created him; male and female he created them.*
> *28 And God blessed them. And God said to them, "Be fruitful and multiply and fill the earth and subdue it, and have dominion over the fish of the sea and over the birds of the heavens and over every living thing that moves on the earth."*

Be fruitful in that you impact your world; multiply in that you reproduce after your kind (the God kind). We are mandated to have dominion in that you exercise godly authority over your world. Any person who achieves these three prongs of the original plan would have lived a fulfilled life. The dictionary definitions of being fulfilled do not adequately explain what it really means to be fulfilled. They fall short by a wide margin. No wonder that many are in therapy or on medication, unable to reconcile in themselves the emptiness they still feel in-spite of all they have acquired and achieved in life. Others resort to a hedonistic lifestyle, abusing their bodies in the quest for fulfilment in life. To many, living a fulfilled life has become an ideal, one that is deeply desired but is painfully unattainable. And that may well be because we lack an understanding of what a fulfilled life is. John 10:10 gives us a clue what the fulfilled life is.

> *John 10:10*
> *The thief comes to steal, kill and destroy, but I have come that they might have life and have it to the full."*

One cannot have an abundance of life, living in fulfilment without having God in one's life. God, Himself is the abundant life. The fulfilled life is not a life lived to one's pleasure and whims but one that is surrendered to God and of benefit to others. That is the life Jesus modelled here on earth. In fact, the fulfilled life is one of sacrifice, a willing conduit through whom the Lord blesses others. Fulfilment does not emanate from doing exactly as one will but doing what the Lord wills. A life that has the stamp of the master's hand on it is one that will benefit this generation and generations yet unborn. That is the fulfilled life!

The logical conclusion then is that my pursuits, achievements, and acquisitions in life will always fail to bring me to the place of deep satisfaction that I seek. This remains the unfortunate truth unless I am aligned in heart and mind with God's original plan. So when God asks the question "can I interrupt your life?", the person of discernment learns to immediately yield to Him. Without His interruptions, life remains a meaningless pursuit. Wealth, fame, great achievements etcetera will continue to fail in filling man's need for a greater purpose. If we want to walk in the favour of God and so live meaningful lives, not only must we welcome His interruptions but we must actively seek them. In this way, we stand to fulfill our God-given assignment of establishing God's kingdom here on earth and our lives reflect His glory. To achieve this, our lives must be completely, not partially under His direction, open and willing.

Let me use the analogy of the relationship between the sun, earth, and moon to explain further what I mean by the fulfilled life being one necessarily of sacrifice and not self – centeredness.

The Earth would be a dismal place without the sun. And the moon would also be just another dull orb if not for the sun's rays. (www.livescience.com)

The earth is representative of the world, the sun used here for the Lord our God, and the moon of each individual whose life is laid open to the use of God to be a blessing to mankind.

The moon shines because its surface reflects light from the sun. And despite the fact that it sometimes seems to shine very brightly, the moon reflects only between 3 and 12 percent of the sunlight that hits it. *(www.livescience.com)*

When we seek for only our good, the gift of life, numerous opportunities presented to us, our gifting and abilities serve only us. To the rest of the world, we may not even exist in that it draws no benefit from these gifting. Our gifting and graces then become hidden under the soot of our self-centeredness and our light does not shine in any meaningful way. When the moon reflects back twelve percent (12%) of the sunlight hitting its surface, it shines brighter than when it reflects three percent (3%) of the sunlight. People are drawn out in admiration of the brightly shining moon and many a couple consider bright moonlight a great addition to a romantic walkabout. In other words, a person's life holds meaning to his generation only inasmuch as they are a conduit channelling God to the world. The moon is glorious only inasmuch as it reflects the sun's light. Otherwise, it is hardly a noticeable orb in the night sky.

In like fashion the glory of God is revealed for all to see - the sun shines on all that dwell on the earth. For many, the heat and light from the sun is something that they soak up willingly and with great enjoyment. These are the "transformers", who seek God and receive directly from Him the unction to function. For others, sunlight is something to be avoided- all too much for the paler constitution. The majority of the human race may sit among this group. For such it is needful, even mandatory, that the moon (children of God) reflect the sunlight, without which there is no authentic source of light other than the "artificialism" of shallow human pursuits. Anything the Lord gives us, including salvation and the opportunity for impact, is not just for our use. We are given all things to benefit the people of our reach. It reveals the hope of God to all those who without the revelation of the power of God in our lives, are doomed to despondency.

God is looking for men and women who will sacrifice everything that the world may know Him. Can God count on you? Can God interrupt your life? Are you willing to put a new perspective on what life is all about?

> *Ezekiel 22:30*
>
> *I searched for a man among them who would build up the wall and stand in the gap before Me for the land that I might not destroy it but I found no one.*

Our world stands in peril when no one stands in the gap before the Lord.

It would take the one who understands, that to sacrifice your life for the good of others is a noble undertaking in the sight of God, to answer this call of God.

Everywhere Jesus went the unction that was upon His life brought the reality of God to the lives of the people. He was a conduit of the grace and mercy of God to all who met Him. In like fashion, we are to be the channels of God's blessing. When people are fearful, full of uncertainty, and wondering where to go, you and I are to point them to the light of God. When people do not know what to do, you and I are to step in to bring hope and direction. In that way, our lives are fulfilled!

The Apostle Paul did not struggle with purpose. His was a life fully yielded to the Lord and so deeply satisfying. As he prepares to depart this world he writes these words that smack fragrantly of a life lived to the full. He had no regrets whatsoever, having been a blessing to his generation. He wrote of his anticipation of the glorious reception of the Lord and the departed saints at his homecoming.

> *2 Timothy 4:7-8*
>
> *7 I have fought the good fight, I have finished the race, I have kept the faith. 8 Now there is in store for me the crown of righteousness, which the Lord, the righteous Judge, will award to me on that day—and not only to me, but also to all who have longed for his appearing.*

What a statement! a testament to the fulfilled life.
It is my prayer that you will receive this blessing; for a life lived in His service and to His plan, is what the Lord calls us to. As you allow Him room in your life, actively seeking His interruptions, may yours be the blessing of the fulfilled life!

May the Lord Interrupt Your Life and make you Impactful!!
May His interruptions take you to greater heights, and bring you to deeper insights in Him. May your generation and those yet to come to know that this one lived and the world knew he/ she did.- Be blessed.

Prayer:

Lord, I pray that you help me identify my assigned place in you, and may I never vacate my post. As you make clear my assignment and show me clearly my sphere of influence, grant unction for effective function. In this, I will be fulfilled. And so Lord, without hesitation or doubt I ask that you interrupt my life, please. For this is the reason I live!

Beloved, if you do not have a relationship with the Lord Jesus then I invite you to accept Him today and secure not just a generation relevant life but an assurance of eternity spent in His presence.

> *Romans 10:9-10 says that "if you declare with your mouth, "Jesus is Lord," and believe in your heart that God raised him from the dead, you will be saved. For it is with your heart that you believe and are justified, and it is with your mouth that you profess your faith and are saved."*

Please say this prayer to give your life to Jesus:
Dear God, I know that I am a sinner and there is nothing that I can do to save myself. I accept that Christ alone is the One who bore my sin when He died on the cross. I believe that He did all that will ever be necessary for me to stand in your holy presence. I ask that you forgive my sins. I accept Jesus as my Lord and saviour and ask Lord that you come into my heart. Thank you for the assurance that you will walk with me. Thank you for hearing this prayer. In Jesus' Name. Amen.

Chapter 7

The Consequence of the delayed response - Attend to your Nineveh!!

Chapter 7

The Consequence of the delayed response - Attend to your Nineveh!!

I sat fuming quietly, agitated within and yet wanting to hold back from speaking. Perhaps my junior colleague had not heard me well as I had instructed her on what care package to put in place for the patient being seen in the maternity triage. I had definitely asked for the patient to be admitted. This patient had a lot of complaints, none of which easily synthesised into a diagnosis. And what is more, she was presenting for the second time within a twenty- four hour period. Good medical practice would indicate admission for both scenarios if they existed in isolation. When coincidentally present in the same patient, it would be quite irresponsible to dismiss her and send such a patient home.

We had no idea what was going on with this lady. Whether it was something medically significant or not, we could not immediately conclude it was safe to send her home.

Was she a victim of domestic violence? That sometimes is a reason why a patient may recurrently present to the hospital. In this situation, they tend to give a string of bizarre symptoms that make diagnosis difficult. Having said that, sometimes the inconsistency of the presenting symptoms may signal a more ominous pathology.

Truth be told I was upset with not one but two junior colleagues. Ironically my upset was not equally distributed towards both colleagues. I was more upset with the junior colleague who had spoken directly to me. It was to her that

I had given concise instructions on the patient's care. For some reason, she had re-discussed the patient with another junior colleague and he had come up with a different plan of management. They both seemed to have completely ignored the two red flags staring us in the face. Nothing made sense out of the presented symptoms and she had come back twice in twenty- four hours.

I wondered why the situation upset me so. Differing opinions in medical practice are commonplace. If one carried the clinical responsibility for the decision made, then you tended to have your opinion deferred to unless in obvious endangering of the patient. That is simply because experience does count for something. As I mulled over it in mind, I could not easily decipher why I felt this patient warranted a second look. No other member of my team felt the same way. I realised that the past fifteen years of medical practice had taught me things not written in any medical textbook. My gut instinct plays a massive role in deciphering what to make of what my patients tell me. In a way, that is a skill that comes with "grey hair", not necessarily adaptable from lectures or books. This was what was telling me that the right thing to do was to have kept that patient in the hospital. I asked my colleagues to contact the patient and offer an apology. Following this they were to invite her back into the hospital, something they went off grudgingly to do.

By the time the patient came back in, her blood test results were back. Upon reviewing these and going through her history yet again, it became apparent that she had acute fatty liver of pregnancy. Thank God I had had her called back in. She could have become very unwell whilst at home. Like many after a hospital visit, she might have failed to re-attend even if her symptoms were beginning to worsen. Often, there is a tendency to try not to be bothersome. This could have had a disastrous outcome. Thank God although grudgingly done, my colleagues did listen in the end. The disaster was thus averted!

As I sat thinking through the events of the shift, I realised something unusual was happening. Usually, the Spirit of the Lord is quick to put me in my proper place when I exhibit the human failings I harbour. The Spirit is quick to point out to me instances of pride, anger, self-centeredness, and unreasonableness. Yet on this occasion when I expected to be reprimanded for being upset, the Spirit began to speak to me about how He feels when I ignore His prompting and leading. It was as if in my displeasure at my instructions being ignored, the Spirit of the Lord sought to teach me a principle for life. He began to unfold the story of Jonah to me in a way that made me realise that, there can be serious consequences when I depart from the leading of the Lord.

I shall endeavour to set out here what the Lord taught me in my internal mulling!

Jonah 1: 1-3
1 Now the word of the LORD came to Jonah the son of Amittai, saying, 2 "Arise, go to Nineveh, that great city, and call out against it, for their evil has come up before me." 3 But Jonah rose to flee to Tarshish from the presence of the LORD. He went down to Joppa and found a ship going to Tarshish. So he paid the fare and went down into it, to go with them to Tarshish, away from the presence of the LORD

The biblical story of Jonah details the account of the journey the prophet Jonah undertook in defiance of God's instructions. It illustrates how sometimes we put our lives and the lives of those around us (family, friends, colleagues etcetera) in jeopardy because of our disobedience. You may wonder how exactly this applies to you. Let us look at it from this angle: someone's opportunity to come to salvation in the Lord is somewhat tied to your obedience, very much akin to the patient safety issues highlighted above. When we fail to act as we should when we should, someone is at the peril of grave danger!

Romans 10:14 in the amplified version helps clarify this.

> *But how are people to call upon Him Whom they have not believed [in Whom they have no faith, on Whom they have no reliance]? And how are they to believe in Him [adhere to, trust in, and rely upon Him] of Whom they have never heard? And how are they to hear without a preacher?*

There are those within your circles whose sole pointer to the Lord Jesus is you. They are awaiting your manifestation as a child of God that they may also know Him. Whilst you look like, talk like, act like and "smell" like the world, there are many individuals who stay blinded to the light of God. Until you step into your true identity as a child of God, you are neither fruitful nor multiplying. You are the city set upon a hill. Yours is to be a shining example of godliness that others may come to God by your example. You are the light and salt of the earth. And so long as your mandate is left unfulfilled, your eternity and theirs are in jeopardy.

Eternity spent outside the presence of God is eternity spent in torment and grief.

You and I are called to be examples unto the world. Working from the premise that human beings are social (gregarious) beings you will rarely find any man living in isolation or as an island. Whether you are conscious of it or not, three things happen to us all as we go through life: We are observed! We are imitated! We in turn imitate and learn from others!

Only psychopaths deviate from this! As tends to be in life, some lead, but others follow. Some serve as examples or models whilst others are happy to imitate. To explain, 'An Example' simply, is a person, action, or thing, that is worthy of imitation. It is a pattern or model, as of something, to be imitated or avoided (can be negative). Generally, if something has the typical features of a particular kind of thing, you can say that it is an example of that kind of thing.

That is to say, you and I, having been mandated to be examples of Christ in this generation, ought to have the typical features of Jesus Christ. Jesus demonstrated attributes of humility, obedience to the will of God, love, faithfulness, and prayerfulness. He was patient, kind, and forgiving. He demonstrated a true hunger for souls. It is only as we demonstrate these attributes that we become a beacon of hope to the world. We become the magnet that draws others unto our God. Unfortunately, in our world today, it often is difficult to differentiate the Christian from the unbeliever. You would note that as Jonah joined the passengers boarding the ship to Tarshish that day, there was nothing that identified him as a man of God. There was nothing in his demeanour that gave him up as a Jew or one who knew Yahweh. He had to be asked for his identity later on. That unfortunately is the status of many who profess Christ in our generation.

The modern-day Christian is often difficult to tell apart from the worldly- neither appearance, speech, nor conduct can be considered as any different from that exhibited by the worldly. I dare to throw a challenge to Christians today!! In your circles of friends and associates, are you an example, a model, and a pacesetter? Or are you an imitator? Are you leading or being led? So long as you name Jehovah as your God, He places a demand on you; that you conduct yourself in a manner worthy of the name you bear.

Where the world sees us as no different from them, we have failed to fulfil our God-given mandate!

> *Romans 2: 17- 24*
>
> *Now you, if you call yourself a Jew; if you rely on the law and boast in God; if you know his will and approve of what is superior because you are instructed by the law; if you are convinced that you are a guide for the blind, a light for those who are in the dark, an instructor of the foolish, a teacher of little children, because you have in the law the embodiment of knowledge and truth— you, then, who teach others, do you not teach yourself? You who preach against stealing, do you steal? You who say that people should not commit adultery, do you commit adultery? You who abhor idols, do you rob temples? You who boast in the law, do you dishonour God by breaking the law?*

> *As it is written: "God's name is blasphemed among the Gentiles because of you."*
> *Circumcision has value if you observe the law, but if you break the law, you have become as though you had not been circumcised. So then, if those who are not circumcised keep the law's requirements, will they not be regarded as though they were circumcised? The one who is not circumcised physically and yet obeys the law will condemn you who, even though you have the written code and circumcision, are a lawbreaker.*

I believe that the Lord looks with mercy and love on the lost world. The day of reckoning will come, but till then His heartbeat is that all men will come to His saving knowledge. The Lord however is greatly displeased when we, who call on His name, put His name in disrepute with our conduct. The clergyman sexually assaulting members of the congregation, little ones who approach in trust of the esteemed position, defiles the Lord's name and His holy place. The Christian wife or husband cheating on the spouse gives room for the world to defame our God. The Lord would, that if you were hot, be hot!

The coldness of spirit is equally a preferred state in His sight than the lukewarm heart and mind. Such, He spits out of His mouth. There is an opportunity now, to step up to your calling, honouring the name of the Lord.

There may be many reasons why we delay in responding to the call of the Lord. Jonah was greatly conflicted about the assignment God set for him concerning the people of Nineveh.

In his opinion, these were a cruel people, not deserving of God's mercy and love. Jonah wanted them punished, not saved. He feared God in His mercy will forgive their sins and not punish their misdeeds. That would be the height of unfairness, in Jonah's eyes.

The people of Nineveh deserved to die for their sins. And yet here was God telling him to go and proclaim His word to them.

There are times when we also are conflicted within. When the Spirit prompts us to extend the mercies and love of God to others, we may sometimes judge them as too sinful to be saved. How do we feel about a known "face" in our community? Do we feel a tug on our heartstrings to help them find God? Or do we steer clear of them, secretly wishing that they will get a just recompense for all their wrongs? In our legalistic claim to holiness, we think sometimes that our righteousness is a result of our own efforts. We forget that grace brought us in and that same grace compels us to reach out to the lost. What a beautiful reminder though that God, through the Apostle Paul sends to us.

> *Ephesians 2:8-9*
>
> *8 For it is by grace you have been saved, through faith—and this is not from yourselves, it is the gift of God—*
> *9 not by works, so that no one can boast.*

He reminds us how we came to salvation that, the mercy shown us might be extended to others. Like Jonah, we may seek to shirk the responsibility to make more of the God kind.

We may seek to do what we will, picking, and choosing the instances of our sharing the gospel of Jesus. Let us be careful though beloved!

> *Acts 2:19 – 21 will have us know the times!!*
>
> *19 I will show wonders in the heavens above and signs on the earth below, blood and fire and billows of smoke. 20The sun will be turned to darkness and the moon to blood before the coming of the great and glorious day of the Lord. 21 And everyone who calls on the name of the Lord will be saved.'*

The current trends we see will suggest that there is no time to waste in reaching out to others for Christ. The earthquakes, epidemics, and pandemic we see; the abject poverty and total disregard for human life and its value, all point to one fact: Jesus is coming back and soon. Attend to your Nineveh lest they perish! There is a consequence to your delayed response. Your inactivity may become the reason why someone dies today without ever finding the Lord.

Jonah fled from before God to Tarshish, a city that lay opposite to the direction to Nineveh. Are you also fleeing the presence of God – calling parallel things as truth in order to fit in? Are you hiding your identity as a child of God by traveling in the opposite direction to His precepts? Are you trying the best you can to avoid speaking out about the impending judgement of God? The world deserves what is coming to them, you might be thinking. The Lord has a different opinion.

He wills that none may perish but how will they know Him unless someone tells them.

That "someone" is you and I, who are the "called out" (the ecclesia) and then sent back to the world to be a lighthouse beckoning all to the safety of the shore.

As Jonah sought to escape his assignment, God sought to reroute him. And what a great storm arose as a result. The ship tossed and groaned under the onslaught of huge waves. So great was the gravity of the situation that the ship was emptied of its cargo into the sea. Yet the ship was still in danger of sinking as the sea did not calm down.

Jonah 1: 4- 11

4 But the LORD hurled a great wind upon the sea, and there was a mighty tempest on the sea, so that the ship threatened to break up. 5 Then the mariners were afraid, and each cried out to his god. And they hurled the cargo that was in the ship into the sea to lighten it for them. But Jonah had gone down into the inner part of the ship and had lain down and was fast asleep. 6 So the captain came and said to him, "What do you mean, you sleeper? Arise, call out to your god! Perhaps the god will give a thought to us, that we may not perish." 7 And they said to one another, "Come, let us cast lots, that we may know on whose account this evil has come upon us." So they cast lots, and the lot fell on Jonah. 8 Then they said to him, "Tell us on whose account this evil has come upon us. What is your occupation? And where do you come from? What is your country?

> *And of what people are you?" 9 And he said to them, "I am a Hebrew, and I fear the LORD, the God of heaven, who made the sea and the dry land." 10 Then the men were exceedingly afraid and said to him, "What is this that you have done!" For the men knew that he was fleeing from the presence of the LORD, because he had told them. 11 Then they said to him, "What shall we do to you, that the sea may quiet down for us?" For the sea grew more and more tempestuous.*

May I be so bold to say, beloved, that some storms raging in your life may be as a result of you running from the presence of God!! The constant struggle to make it in your chosen career field may be a result of your refusal to listen to the leading of the Spirit. Before you ever were, God had already planned your days. It is intriguing that the clay now thinks to tell the potter what better to make it into. Sometimes the only way to a reset of purposes, to fulfil destiny is a royal shakedown. Where the Lord renders us defenceless and anchor-less, we find our trembling way back to Him. With tremulousness comes a recognition of the divine authority and sovereignty of the Lord over our lives. When the Lord chooses to batter down our battlements and crumble our castles of refuge, we somehow find our way back to Him.

Jonah was fleeing from the presence of the Lord but found himself in the presence of the almighty. He found himself helpless, where neither money nor social contacts could be of any help to him. But even then, he preferred to die than be used as an instrument in the salvation of the people of Nineveh. He preferred to be thrown overboard than head to Nineveh. He could just have easily said, turn the ship around, and set course for Nineveh. Instead, he said," chuck me into the sea". Such was his determination to run from God!! In many ways, we act like Jonah. We would rather be caught dead than have our friends think lesser of us. We are much more comfortable to sit on the seat of scoffers than raise an admonishing finger to halt evil conversation. We prefer to leave than serve in what we consider a menial position in the church. There is no glory in cleaning pews! If I cannot be offered the opportunity to demonstrate my skills of oratory in the pulpit before the whole congregation, how dare you ask me to clean or usher others in. And so like Jonah, we choose to not be involved at all.

> *Jonah 1:12 - 15*
> *12 He said to them, "Pick me up and hurl me into the sea; then the sea will quiet down for you, for I know it is because of me that this great tempest has come upon you." 13 Nevertheless, the men rowed hard to get back to dry land, but they could not, for the sea grew more and more tempestuous against them. 14 Therefore they called out to the LORD, "O LORD, let us not perish for this man's life, and lay not on us innocent blood, for you, O LORD, have done as it pleased you." 15 So they picked up Jonah and hurled him into the sea, and the sea ceased from its raging.*

At Jonah's own instigation he was thrown overboard into the sea. The Lord could have abandoned Jonah but He was not done yet with Jonah. In the same way, the Lord is not done with you. He is giving you the opportunity yet again to step up to the plate and be His ambassador. He is repeatedly knocking at the door of our hearts, asking " can I interrupt your life?"

Would you consider letting Him in? Get to beloved! Attend to your Nineveh! Being thrown into the ocean was certain death but because the Lord had other plans for Jonah's life, God rescued him. Being thrown into the sea was just the push Jonah needed to refocus his attention on God's purpose for him. The reality is that he could have died had the Lord not intervened.

> *Jonah 1:17*
>
> *And the LORD appointed a great fish to swallow up Jonah. And Jonah was in the belly of the fish three days and three nights.*

Many times we face dangerous situations that solely arise because of our stubborn attitude before God. Being in the whale is synonymous with being entombed. Sometimes we run the risk of both a physical and spiritual death as we seek to flee from His presence. But thanks be to God for His bowels of mercy. Thanks be to the most high for His grace which most times pulls us back from the brink of the grave. We ought to be careful not to abuse this grace of God. We may never again have the chance to redeem the numerous opportunities we let slip by. There is but one letter differentiating grace from the grave.

Finally, in despair, Jonah found himself ready to reset to his calling. He cried unto Jehovah God from a changed heart. And the Lord heard his prayer.

> *And the LORD spoke to the fish, and it vomited Jonah out upon the dry land. (Jonah 2:10, ESV)*

Back on dry land, Jonah went on to preach to the people of Nineveh who turned to the Lord, forsaking their wicked ways. Beloved Jonah had a second chance but you and I may not be so blessed. The Lord calls for your attention now. The Lord seeks to interrupt your life now. Obedience is attended by His blessing. Disobedience to the call comes with a grave cost – three days of being blotted from the presence of God.

> *Here is a revelation for yet another time!!! Remember with God one day is as a thousand years and a thousand years as one day. Let him that has an ear hear that which the spirit says!!*

Patients die when doctors fail to perceive them in depth. Souls perish when they that are sent fail to attend to their ministry. May you never again lose the opportunity to respond to God's call- the lives of others depend on it. Get to! Attend to your Nineveh!! And may the Lord bless you as you yield yourself for His use.

Prayer

Psalm 139:7-12

7 Where can I go from your Spirit? Where can I flee from your presence? 8 If I go up to the heavens, you are there; if I make my bed in the depths, you are there 9 If I rise on the wings of the dawn, if I settle on the far side of the sea, 10 even there your hand will guide me, your right hand will hold me fast. 11 If I say, "Surely the darkness will hide me and the light become night around me," 12 even the darkness will not be dark to you; the night will shine like the day, for darkness is as light to you.

Lord, I acknowledge that you are sovereign. I cannot run from your presence and will no longer seek to do so. I understand the gravity of my failure to answer your call. So I give myself over to you. I pray that you may find me useful in your vineyard. May I by example and by word, draw others to your steadfast love.

CAN GOD INTERRUPT YOUR LIFE?

Glossary

*Anointing: the work of the Holy Spirit to set apart a person, place, or thing for divine use. It empowers people to accomplish God's work.

* Bible: a collection of religious texts or scriptures sacred to Christians, who generally consider the Bible to be a product of divine inspiration and a record of the relationship between God and humans.

* Blastocyst: a stage in the developing baby's life where it is made up of an inner group of cells with an outer shell. The inner group of cells will become the baby with the outer group of cells will become the "membranes.
* DNA: a substance that carries genetic information in the cells of plants and animals.

* Diagnosis: identification of the nature of an illness or other problem by examination of the symptoms.

* Embryo and foetus: the unborn offspring in the process of development, from approximately the second to the eighth week after fertilisation (after which it is usually termed a foetus).

* Forceps: an instrument for grasping, holding firmly, or exerting traction upon objects especially for delicate operations (as by jewellers or surgeons).

- Forceps are smooth, curved metal instruments that look like large tongs. They're placed around the baby's head to help pull the baby out.

* Full-time Ministry: the work or vocation of a minister of religion.

* Gametes: special cells in the human body needful to make a baby (ovum [egg] from the woman, sperm from the man).

* Graces: virtue coming from God, special divinely given abilities.

* Incubation: the process of keeping something at the right temperature and under the right conditions so it can develop.

* Jesus: The second person of the Trinity, God in human form.

* Kindred/ kin: one's family and relations

* Martyr: a person who sacrifices something of great value and especially life itself for the sake of God or principle.

* Ministry: an activity carried out by Christians to express or spread their faith, the prototype being the Great Commission.

* Morula: a solid ball of cells (usually 6-12 cells), resulting from division of a fertilised ovum

* Nuclei (singular nucleus): the central portion of a cell containing all the genetic information of the organism.

* Obstetrics and Gynaecology: a branch (specialty) of medicine that deals with women's health.

* Pathology: the science of the causes and effects of diseases.

* Pharisee: a member of an ancient Jewish sect, distinguished by strict observance of the traditional and written law, and commonly held to have pretensions to superior sanctity.

* Prognosis: a forecast of the likely outcome of a situation.

* Redeem/ Redemption: the action of saving or being saved from sin, error, or evil.

* Specialty Registrar: a grade of doctor practising independently in a given specialty or branch of medicine, but below consultant level.

* The Flesh: a metaphor to describe sinful tendencies.

* The World: the term often connotes the concept of the fallen and corrupt order of human society.

* Unction: interchangeably used with anointing, denoting a state of carrying something of God that makes for effective ministry.

* Ventouse: a cup-shaped suction device that can be attached to a baby's head to help them to be born. You might have heard it called a vacuum delivery.

* Zygote: initial cell containing the full genetic material from both parents, formed by a fertilisation event between two gametes.

*Acute fatty liver of pregnancy (AFLP): Some women develop a type of fatty liver in the final trimester (last three months) of their pregnancy. Often symptoms of AFLP are non-specific and can be mistaken for another condition, making early diagnosis difficult.

*Amoxicillin: An antibiotic belong to the penicillin group of medicines.

*Conduit: a natural or artificial channel through which something (such as a fluid) is conveyed.

*Damascus: The city in the Biblical story which Paul was travelling to, to stop people believing in Jesus Christ when hears the voice of God. The experience makes him become a Christian. Damascus may also describe an experience that completely changes the way that you think about something.

*Incarnation: A central Christian doctrine that God became flesh, assumed a human nature and became a man in the form of Jesus Christ, the Son of God and the second person of the Trinity. Christ was truly God and truly man.

*Kidney dish: a shallow basin with a kidney-shaped base and sloping walls used to receive soiled dressings and other medical waste.

*Mosaic Law: traditionally the first five books of the Hebrew Bible are attributed to Moses who led Israel out of Egypt. The law attributed to Moses, specifically the laws set out in the books of Leviticus and Deuteronomy, as a consequence came to be considered supreme over all other sources of authority (any king and/or his officials), and the Levites were the guardians and interpreters of the law.

*Sponge holding forceps: a medical instrument used for holding cleaning swabs.

*Stethoscope: a medical instrument for listening to the action of someone's heart or breathing or bowel sounds.

NOTES

Printed in Great Britain
by Amazon